# Career Express

## Business English — B2

### Teacher's Book

Kenneth Thomson

Adviser
Dr Peter Tischer

UNIVERSITY OF SUSSEX

SCLS

LLC LANGUAGE TUTOR REFERENCE

*Garnet*
EDUCATION

# Credits

**Published by**
Garnet Publishing Ltd
8 Southern Court
South Street
Reading RG1 4QS, UK

www.garneteducation.com

Copyright © Cornelsen Verlag GmbH, Berlin 2010

The right of Kenneth Thomson to be identified as the author of this work has been asserted by him in accordance with the Copyright, Designs and Patents Act 1988.

All rights reserved.

No part of this publication may be reproduced, stored in a retrieval system, or transmitted in any form or by any means, electronic, mechanical, photocopying, recording or otherwise, without the prior permission of the Publisher. Any person who does any unauthorized act in relation to this publication may be liable to criminal prosecution and civil claims for damages.

This edition is not to be sold in Austria, Germany or Switzerland.

First edition 2013
ISBN: 978 1 90757 570 9

British Library Cataloguing-in-Publication Data
A catalogue record for this book is available from the British Library.

Every effort has been made to trace copyright holders and we apologize in advance for any unintentional omissions. We will be happy to insert the appropriate acknowledgements in any subsequent editions.

**Production**
Editor: Kathrin Köller, Martin Moore, Clare Roberts
Freelance editor: Rani Kumar
Design and layout: Sabine Theuring, Simon Ellway

**Printed and bound** in Lebanon by International Press: interpress@int-press.com

# Table of Contents

| Career Express Business English B2 | 4 |
| --- | --- |
| Career Express Business English B2 Online | 7 |
| Career Express Business English B2 Teacher's Book | 8 |

| Unit 1 | Applying for an internship | 12 |
| --- | --- | --- |
| Unit 2 | Work and p(l)ay | 21 |
| Unit 3 | Customer service | 27 |
| Unit 4 | Selling to the consumer | 33 |
| Unit 5 | Globalization and international trade | 39 |
| Unit 6 | Products and production | 47 |
| Unit 7 | Marketing communications | 53 |
| Unit 8 | Debts, savings and investments | 61 |
| Unit 9 | Company structure | 69 |
| Unit 10 | Accounting | 77 |
| Unit 11 | Rapidly developing economies | 85 |
| Unit 12 | Starting a business | 93 |

| Photocopiable activities | 100 |
| --- | --- |

## Symbols and terms in the Teacher's Book

 Key or suggested answer for the exercise

 Audio track on CD 1

 Audio track on CD 2

 Photocopiable activity in the appendix

 Video clip(s) online

 Exercise suited to pair work

 Exercise suited to group work

# Introduction

## Career Express Business English B2

The increase in the number of students required to learn English as a component of Business Studies courses in universities has resulted in demand for a "one stop" business English Course Book to meet these students' needs.

*Career Express Business English B2*, a multimedia course which aims at improving the English of students at the B2 level of the CEF (Common European Framework), has been tailored to meet the precise language needs of Business Studies students both for their studies and their future careers. The aim of the Course Book is to equip students with concrete professional skills which are firmly focussed on the job market. Also in keeping with the vocational focus of business courses, *Career Express Business English B2* will assist students in developing key "soft" skills, namely competence in team work and intercultural awareness.

*Career Express Business English B2* goes well beyond the confines of other Course Books in a number of ways.

Firstly, the range of topics covered by the Course Book reflects the full scope of students' study. Finance and accounting, production, business organization, marketing, sales and customer service are covered in detail. Further, these topics are considered in the context of current business imperatives; a context furnished by units which examine globalization and rapidly developing economies and the challenges posed by these to existing models of achieving profitability. Not only does *Career Express Business English B2* complement the range of the students' studies and give them the wherewithal to discuss this in English, but it also builds upon and gives them practice in core academic skills such as paraphrasing and note taking in English.

The choice of topics reflects the range of students' studies as well as their personal needs regarding their professional development. Students required to undertake an internship abroad as part of their course of study will be equipped to put themselves in the best position to secure the internship of their choice by Unit 1 *Applying for an internship*. The Course Books accompanies students in their development from first work experience through to considering whether they are cut out to become entrepreneurs, a choice which will be pursued by a significant number of your students and considered by many more in the course of their studies, in the final unit.

Secondly, *Career Express Business English B2* addresses students' need for the fundamental, "nuts and bolts" lexis of specific business topics. The lexis featured in each unit is the result of careful analysis of the most frequently occurring and useful vocabulary: the Course Books takes a "lean" approach to lexis, providing that which is of clear use to students and which they will be able to pick up and run with immediately. It will not burden them with the task of having to weed out language which will not be of direct use to them.

Along with providing sector-specific lexis in this targeted fashion, *Career Express Business English B2* goes on to consider the broader sweep of the topics it covers. Unit 10 *Accounting* illustrates this well. The unit provides students with the full set of technical language they will need to discuss financial statements and integrates this into discussion of recent major accounting frauds and the changes in regulation for financial reporting which have resulted from this.

The result of this two-fold approach to the topics covered by the Course Book is that students will have the necessary language to function on a day-to-day basis at work along with the English skills necessary to articulate the "bigger issues" regarding specific business topics.

Thirdly, and in line with the expectations and study practices of the target group, the Course Book offers a multimedia environment for learning business English which exceeds the boundaries of more conventional course books. In addition to encouraging students to take responsibility for their own learning in part by directing them to undertake internet research on specific issues, *Career Express Business English B2* integrates videos and online *Self Study* material which reinforce key aspects of the Course Book's units.

# Introduction

## Unit overview

Each unit of *Career Express Business English B2* consists of a number of key elements which are balanced to present students with the opportunity to examine the unit's topic from a number of perspectives, as well as investigate and practise the lexis attached to the unit. In order to help students gain a swift overview of its content, each unit also begins with an information box providing a summary of the topics and skills which will be focussed upon as well as highlights of the online *Self Study* exercises related to the unit. Further reference is made to *Self Study* exercises throughout the units where exercises appropriate to various points in a unit are clearly indicated on the page.

In the four units which are supplemented by a video, details of this are also provided here.

## Listening

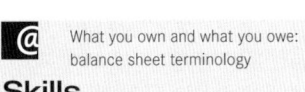

Listenings, which play a key role in *Career Express Business English B2*, though they are on occasion used to provide the backbone to warm up discussions, frequently elucidate on and offer fresh perspectives about topics which students have already covered in their reading. The listenings in *Career Express Business English B2* are designed to pose students with a challenge. They are often complex in nature as are the accompanying listening tasks. Moreover, they expose students to a variety of native and non-native speaker accents and English spoken at a natural speed.

The listenings featured in the Course Book are not only authentic in terms of the language deployed in them but also in terms of their length: listening exercises in *Career Express Business English B2* have been designed to train students' powers of comprehension over relatively long periods of time, thus developing additionally their stamina when listening to English. The Course Book comes complete with two CDs containing all the listenings, a feature which offers students the chance to listen to the audio tracks once again after the lesson.

## Reading

Every unit contains reading texts which elaborate on the unit's topic focus. The aim here has been to provide students with as many authentic texts as possible: texts contained in the Course Book have frequently been sourced from specialist business books, periodicals and websites and offer students exposure to contemporary commentary on the range of business topics covered. The authentic nature of the texts contained in *Career Express Business English B2* underlines the Course Book's emphasis on equipping students for the real world: grappling with authentic texts – and therefore the authentic language of business thinkers – instantly puts students into a realistic context, one which they will repeatedly have to operate in as professionals after university.

The reading texts are long and demanding, allowing students ample opportunity to hone their reading skills. Further, the exercises which accompany texts go well beyond conventional who-why-what comprehension questioning and invite students to explore the lexis and ideas featured in detail.

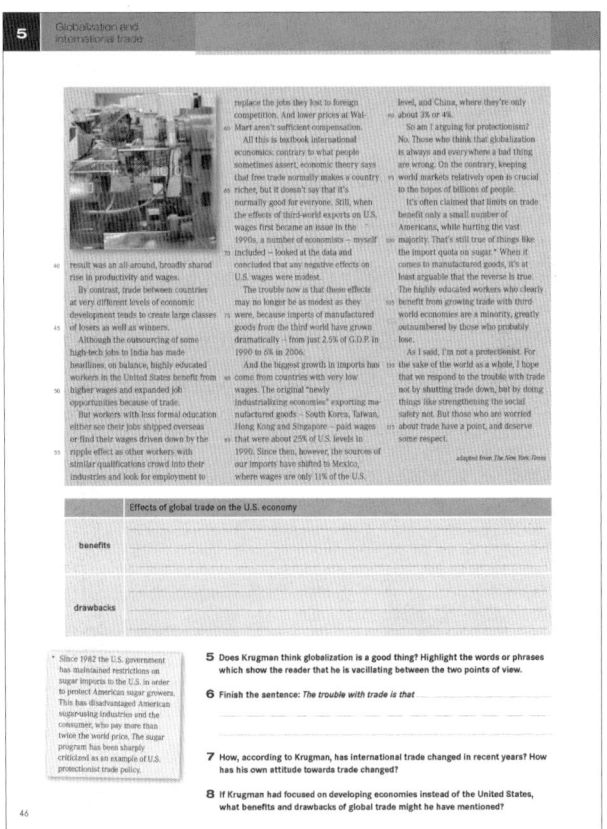

# Introduction

## Business Skills

The second part of each unit is comprised of the *Business Skills* section. Here the unit's topic of focus is complemented by a series of activities dovetailed to it, the aim of which is to equip students with a skill they will need in their professional lives: writing a resumé, giving a presentation, writing emails, describing the key features of products. Students are encouraged to explore the lexis and functional language associated with the skill they are examining through reading, listening and discussion before practising it in role-plays.

## Role-play

*Role-plays* are a pivotal element of the strategy adopted in the *Business Skills* section: they provide the realistic setting in which students get the chance to put into practice the language skills they have been developing in the preceding pages.

*Role-plays* in *Career Express Business English B2* are finely honed to present students with all the information they need to carry them out productively.

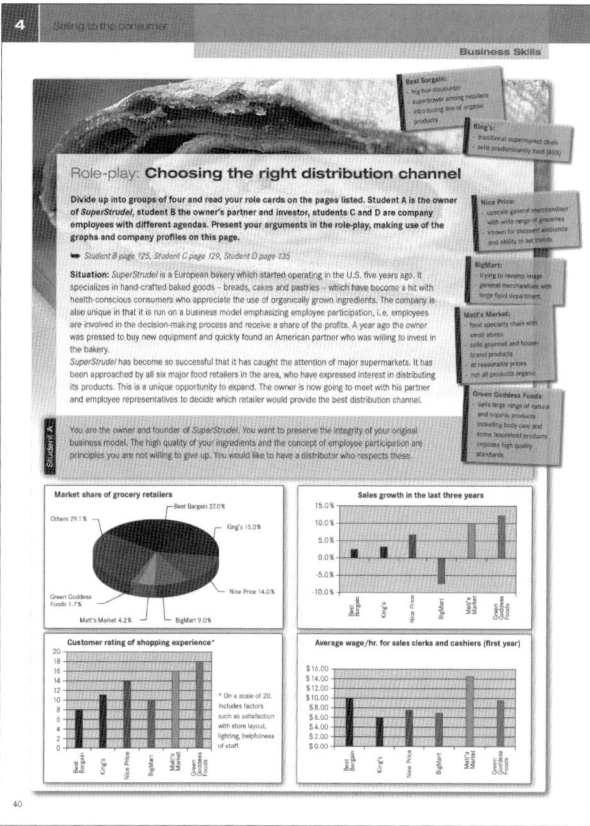

## Diversity

*Career Express Business English B2* pays consistent attention to the intercultural aspects of the topics it covers. Several units in the Course Book take this further by featuring *Diversity* boxes which provide additional insight into cultural divergence regarding the topics at hand and have an accompanying task for students. On occasion, the *Diversity* rubric is incorporated into one of the unit's constant features. For instance, the role-play in Unit 5, which examines differences in how small talk is viewed between cultures, is contextualized in this way.

The result of the consistent attention which is paid by *Career Express Business English B2* to diversity in attitudes and habits between cultures will ensure that students are optimally prepared for work in the globalized economy.

## Company Case

The classroom component of each unit concludes with the *Company Case*. These case studies, directly linked to a unit's topic, encourage students to put on their "managers' hats" and examine the implications of the issues covered in the unit from the perspective of a company.

The emphasis of these case studies is on problem-solving: a challenge relating to the unit's topic faced by a company is presented in a reading text; students are offered the opportunity to analyze this through group discussion before presenting their solution to the other students in the class.

The case studies ensure that the emphasis of units – after the wide-ranging discussions which they encourage about a topic – is anchored in the "real world" realities faced by businesses.

## Over to you

A key concept which underpins the thinking behind *Career Express Business English B2* is that students should take ownership of their own learning. In line with this, the closing two pages of each unit are comprised of the *Over to you* section. On these pages students are presented with the opportunity to carry out further research on an aspect of the unit's topic, do some additional reading comprehension work or complete further exercises focussing on lexis.

Though the intention is that students work on these pages on their own initiative outside of class, the *Over to you* sections offer many activities which you may choose to focus on by setting them as assignments and returning to them in the next class.

# Introduction

## Career Express Business English B2 Online

The extent of the course offered by *Career Express Business English B2* doesn't end with the Course Book but is complemented by Career Express' multimedia component provided by its website.

### Self Study

Each unit is complemented by the "digital workbook" provided on the website. Here students will get the chance to carry out additional exercises on the key grammatical, lexical and business skill elements of each unit. The exercises are presented in a variety of interesting, interactive formats, including listening exercises, which give students the chance to develop their language skills. A key benefit of this component of *Career Express* is that the important groundwork required for improving students' English is covered by students in their own time: *Career Express* offers students abundant practice in the form of interactive exercises while at the same time allowing them to get on with developing their communicative skills when in the classroom.

### Tests

Each unit is also accompanied by an online test which students can use to assess their progress in a unit's grammar, lexis and business skill after having completed the workbook.

### Videos

*Career Express Business English B2* is unique in that it comes with a specially produced video which takes the form of a "business soap opera". The video course *An internship abroad* follows the progress of Rebecca, a business student, who succeeds in applying for an internship with a sports-event company in New York and encounters the typical situations of attending an interview, making a presentation, participating in a meeting and socializing. The four video clips – which topically accompany four units of the Course Book – provide students with examples of authentic business language and provide pointers on useful strategies in the situations which Rebecca is confronted with. All this takes place in the context of a "must watch", soap opera format that students will be comfortable with. Of course, the main reason that students will watch the video avidly is that its main protagonist is in the same position that they may find themselves in. Rebecca is out there on her own and the strategies for coping which she develops can be adopted by students.

### Additional features of the Career Express website for students

In addition to the features already discussed, the website offers students the facility either to hear all the listenings from the Course Book again online or to download them in MP3 format. The website also provides students with a series of useful templates: there are, for instance, templates for writing CVs or drafting the agenda of a meeting.

# Introduction

## Career Express Business English B2 Teacher's Book

Comprehensive as it is, the package offered by *Career Express Business English B2* to students and teachers does not end there. The Course Book and its accompanying online components are complimented by this *Teacher's Book*.

The *Teacher's Book* co-ordinates the wide range of material presented by *Career Express Business English B2* and advises how exercises and activities can best be put into action in your classes allowing students – and their English – to get the most out of the experience.

### Unit contents

Each unit of the *Teacher's Book* begins with two information boxes. The first of these provides a complete overview of the *Self Study* material which accompanies the unit in the online workbook: precise details of the content of the three grammar, vocabulary and business skills exercises as well as the two reading exercises are provided here. In Units 1, 5, 7, and 9, which are accompanied by installments of the video *An internship abroad*, details of this are also provided here.

The box *At a glance* which begins each unit is a concise description of what the unit contains and features some of the key vocabulary which students can expect to encounter in the unit, allowing you to prepare for dealing with this in class. For the benefit of teachers who would like to do some background reading on the unit's topic before going into class, this information box also features suggestions for websites which provide either a concise overview of the topic, more in depth insight into specific aspects of the topic or a source of regular news updates relevant to the topic area.

However, background information provided for teachers to make their job easier doesn't end here in the *Teacher's Book*. Concise information about technical or intercultural aspects of the units are to be found throughout the guide wherever teachers need some backup to put them on a surer footing in the classroom.

Each unit of the Course Book is dealt with in a clear, chronological fashion by the *Teacher's Book*. There are suggestions for how to approach each exercise which include warm-up activities where appropriate. The emphasis here is upon exploiting to the full the potential of exercises to provide opportunities for your students to communicate with one another. Though *Career Express Business English B2* has been designed so that much of the necessary but mechanical practice which students require can be undertaken by them in their own time in the *Self Study* area of the website, conventional exercises – for example, gap fills – do come up in Course Book units where they are necessary. Wherever appropriate in such instances, the *Teacher's Book* makes suggestions about how exercises of this type can be turned into communicative classroom activities, for example, by introducing pairwork or turning exercises into classroom quizzes.

Of course, you may decide not to have your students tackle all the exercises in the Course Book during class time. This may be particularly the case where students are required to undertake fairly long pieces of writing. The *Teacher's Book* aims to help you make the best use of the limited time you have with your students and advises which exercises might best be completed as homework. Ever with an eye to the dictates of the clock, the *Teacher's Book* also makes suggestions about the time that you should allocate to each exercise in the classroom. In cases where exercises are assigned as homework, it makes suggestions about what form assessment of students' homework might take – correction by you or by peers – and how the homework might be fed into the next lesson.

Students are on occasion required to carry out internet research in *Career Express Business English B2*. Wherever possible, the *Teacher's Book* suggests websites that you can direct their attention to in order that students can undertake their research in a focussed and profitable way.

Each unit of the *Teacher's Book* also includes comprehensive answer keys: in the instances where exercises in the Course Book are presented graphically – for example, in tabular or graph form – wherever possible the related answer key appears in the same form, ensuring ease of use. Moreover, on the occasions when there are no right answers to an exercise – students are asked, for instance, to express an opinion based on some data – keys with model answers are provided.

# Introduction

## The role of reading texts

Reading texts play a pivotal role in *Career Express Business English B2* and an appropriate amount of space is given over in each unit of the *Teacher's Book* to suggesting how they might be handled in order that students get the most out of them. Included here are suggestions about how to prepare students before reading as well as pointers about exploiting texts further once the Course Book exercises which accompany them have been completed.

Students reading in a second language can often be tempted to pore over texts and try to understand ever word featured in them. Even experienced language learners have to be reminded of the unnaturalness of this approach – it's almost certainly not how they approach reading in their first language – and have their confidence in their ability to read in different ways in English boosted. This is a primary focus of the *Teacher's Book* which offers suggestions as to whether individual texts might best be skim read for an overview of content or scan read in order to find specific information. The *Teacher's Book* also provides guidance as to which pieces of vocabulary from texts students may need explained to them and how this might in each case be carried out to best advantage. Wherever appropriate, the *Teacher's Book* also suggests how specific texts might be exploited as communicative activities, for instance, by splitting reading between different students turning texts into information gap activities.

## Using listenings in the classroom

The role played by listenings in *Career Express Business English B2* is also an important one. As well as being used to "thicken" the context which has already been created by reading, listenings are frequently used in the Course Book to introduce topics and provide students with the initial lexis, information and setting they require for their discussions. The approaches to listenings suggested by the *Teacher's Book* vary depending on the role played by individual listenings in the build-up of a unit. Suggestions about how to tackle listenings are also contingent on their individual length and complexity. So, where necessary, the *Teacher's Book* contains suggestions about how students might best be prepared for listening, such as brainstorming what is already known about a given topic. Further, advice about how to break up particularly long listenings is also included. On some occasions when students are required to notice specific lexis used in a listening, photocopiable activities have been designed to provide them with the means to do this. Finally, there are frequent suggestions in the *Teacher's Book* about how to extend the scope of discussion generated by a listening, for instance, in the form of additional questions which might be put to students.

## Teaching with video

This *Teacher's Book* is accompanied by a video course online – a unique feature of *Career Express Business English B2* - and can be accessed by students on the *Career Express* website. Though the episodes are primarily intended to be viewed by students in their own time, they can also be used as exciting additions to your classes. In the four units - 1, 5, 7 and 9 – to which the episodes are topically linked, the *Teacher's Book* makes comprehensive suggestions as to how you might best achieve this. Included here is advice about preparing students for viewing, questions which will help direct their viewing as well as questions about Rebecca's performance which they can consider while viewing.

Of course, the pointers about how to deploy the video installments in your classroom contained in the *Teacher's Book* are just suggestions. You may decide you want to use the video in different ways. Here, then, are some further suggestions which might assist you in this.

You might try playing a short section of an installment without sound and ask the students to speculate about what the protagonists are saying. The idea is to elicit phrases from the students which they would expect might be used in such a context. They then get the chance to check their speculations against the video. The idea is to reinforce their existing knowledge, then supplement it with other phrases. Should you do this, be sure to set the scene for your students who will need at least a basic contextual framework upon which to base their speculations. Be sure also to play the scene again with sound so that students can check their speculations against what actually takes place in the video.

You might decide to pause the video at a point of your choosing and ask students to speculate about what happens next. How might the protagonists react to what has just taken place and what might they say?

An extension of this, which you might indulge in should you feel you and your students have the time, would be to suggest that students work in groups to write the script for the scene following the point at which you paused: this could, of course, be set as homework. If you choose to do this, be sure to set aside enough time for the students to act out their scripts in front of the class.

# Introduction

## Role-plays and Company Cases

A good deal of space in the *Teacher's Book* is given over to describing how best to set up the units' *Role-plays* and *Company Cases*. Both of these are important elements of all units: *Role-plays* provide students with an opportunity to put into action key lexis which they have encountered in the unit; the *Company Cases* provides them with a platform upon which they can display their ability to work together to find solutions to problems and think outside the box. In order to maximize the benefit to students of both these activities, careful preparation is required. The *Teacher's Book* provides pointers about how to do this which are specific to each *Role-play* and *Company Case*.

## Over to you

The *Over to you* section at the end of each unit is clearly intended for students to work on in their own time. Nevertheless, each of these sections contains interesting activities, including, for example, internet research and writing assignments, which you will probably want to ensure your students complete and the results of which can be fed into later lessons. The *Teacher's Book* identifies the aspects of each *Over to you* section the results of which could be covered in the next lesson and provides practical suggestions as to the ways in which students could be directed to complete these. In the case of internet research, the guide provides website addresses that the students can use in their search for information. Where the research to be undertaken is fairly extensive, the *Teacher's Book* suggests divisions of labor among students which will ensure that they can individually look into their area of concern in some detail while contributing to a "big picture" created by the efforts of the whole class. Regarding writing assignments, the *Teacher's Book* suggests additional advice that could be given to students about how to structure their writing as well as pointers as to how this can be incorporated into the next class.

*Over to you* sections frequently also provide students with additional reading which is related to the topic of the unit. The *Teacher's Book* contains advice as to how you might encourage your students to undertake this extra reading by pointing out to them the ways in which it complements what they have learned in the units.

## Photocopiable activities

Each unit of this *Teacher's Book* contains photocopiable activities which pick up on key aspects of lexis from each unit and give you the option of offering your students further practice should you feel this is necessary. Even if you feel that your students don't require further practice, the photocopiable activities provide, in addition, interesting communicative settings which students can use to boost their fluency.

The photocopiable activities, which take many different forms ranging from board and card games, to matching exercises to text sorting and analyzing activities, are fitted in to the most appropriate points of the units and offer the additional benefit of allowing students a short "breather" from the environment of the Course Book. The *Teacher's Book* also contains comprehensive notes which explain how the photocopiable activities can be put into action in the classroom: where appropriate, these notes are accompanied by answer keys.

## The modern, multimedia classroom

*Career Express Business English B2* has been designed to meet the needs of students whose conception of study is at least as much informed by the internet and associated communication technologies as it is by the conventional textbook: hence the emphasis in *Career Express* of presenting students with a multimedia learning experience.

The *Teacher's Book* frequently suggests ways of harnessing communication technologies in the classroom.

Here are some suggestions as to how you might achieve this.

If you have a digital camera and laptop, bring them to every lesson. You may spontaneously decide, for instance, that you want to video a series of student presentations. In short, having the ability to go online in the classroom will enable you to respond flexibly to a variety of situations which arise during lessons.

Encourage your students to bring laptops with them to lessons if they have them. Again this will enable a flexible response to any sudden needs for research which arise. If students have mobile access to the internet, they can look for information – or research lexis – online as the need arises. Moreover, should you spontaneously decide that your students do indeed need some additional grammar practice, they can be carrying this out in the students' area of the Career Express website within a couple of minutes.

If your institution has an LMS (Learning Management System) you will be able to use it to deliver multimedia content to students. You may decide, for instance, that your class would benefit from listening to a news report relating to a unit topic. Many broadcasters make news segments available for download as MP3 files. The BBC, to take the most notable

# Introduction

example, has a large archive of such material which is constantly updated: business news podcasts, for instance, can be sourced at http://www.bbc.co.uk/podcasts/series/wbnews. Having downloaded a news report you want your students to concentrate on, you can distribute it to your class – or several classes at once – via LMS.

Another advantage of using LMS to distribute materials you want to use in the classroom is that you can monitor who has actually accessed it. In the event, for instance, of some students not having looked at a piece of material which will be crucial for your next class, you can send them a reminder to do so thus ensuring that everybody comes fully prepared to the lesson.

LMS will also allow for a high degree of interaction between students out of class time. Most systems enable forums and chat. The potential uses of these functions are clear. For instance, students could use the chat function to help them plan a joint assignment outside of class or start a forum discussion about a particular issue that has arisen during class.

This "always on" use of communication technology will be in line with your students' expectations and in keeping with many of the suggestions about how to get the best out of *Career Express Business English B2* which are made in this *Teacher's Book*.

# Applying for an internship

## Self Study

**Vocabulary**
- Using the right adjectives when marketing yourself
- Word families for job hunting
- Action verbs for the job-hunt

**Grammar**
- Talking about your skills
- Capitalization
- The role of tenses in career talk

**Skills**
- Structuring a letter of application
- Resumé writing
- Talking about your achievements

**Reading**
- Understanding job adverts
- Key words in job adverts

**Video**
- Preparing for an interview
- Dealing with tough job interview questions
- Good job interview answers 1
- Good job interview answers 2
- A candidate's USPs

## At a glance

This opening unit of **Career Express Business English B2** will be of immediate benefit to students by preparing them for an internship abroad which they might need to undertake to fulfill their course requirements or for their careers.

The unit deals with its topic in logical order. From identifying potentially interesting internship programs to writing **cover letters** and **resumés** to presenting themselves in **interviews**, the latter points being dealt with in a "hands on" manner in the unit's *Business Skills* section. The unit will also help students to understand the importance of putting themselves in the position of **recruiters** and establishing what their expectations are. In this context, conceptualizing a resumé so that it really stands out is covered in some depth. Additionally, students encounter key adjectives and action verbs with which to enliven their **job applications**. The unit's *Over to you* section offers them the chance to evaluate their personal strengths and weaknesses in a SWOT analysis.

Unit 1 also features a video component – designed specifically for students in higher education - starring a student coping with an interview situation in the United States.

The following website will provide your students with easily digestible information about the steps involved in applying for internships:
http://www.howtodothings.com/education/a4193-how-to-apply-for-an-internship.html

## Warm-up

Divide your students into small groups and ask them to read the advertisement. They should then spend five minutes discussing the internship in their groups, saying whether it would be of interest to them personally and giving reasons for this. When the time is up, bring the class back together and ask two or three students to report briefly their assessments of the *American Fields* internship.

Now set the groups a further task. Each student should think about the type of internship they would personally like to undertake, taking into consideration aspects such as industry or sector, the size of the company, which business functions they would like to familiarize themselves with, the duration of the internship and its location. They should then describe this to the other group members. When this discussion is over, round off by asking a few students to each pick another student from their group and recount what each said about their personal preferences for an internship.

# Applying for an internship

## Listening: Finding an internship

**1** Before they start discussing these questions in their groups, tell your students that their collective aim here will be to come up with a list of pointers about finding internships to apply for because they are going to pool their collective experience. Ask them to spend more time discussing the first question than the latter and set them a five-minute time limit.

Now consolidate their ideas on the board. Get the students to call out the results of their discussions and write these up to form a checklist of useful tips for finding internships. If necessary, supplement the students' suggestions with some of your own.

Your students might come up with the following suggestions about ways to find internships:
Newspapers, job websites and university career notice boards often contain advertisements for internships and are certainly worth a look.

**2** If you judge that your students will be in the position to complete this exercise relatively easily, liven it up by turning it into a quick quiz. Each group is a team and you play the role of the quiz master. Read each word in the left-hand column in turn, allowing team members time to read and confer. For more able students you may wish to set a time limit for this stage, such as 30 seconds. The first team to say *ready* can attempt to make the match and read out the definition they think fits. Should they get this wrong, give the other teams another chance to answer. The team with the most correct answers wins.

Extend the exercise by handing out copies of a transcript key such as the one that can be found here: www.rochester.edu/registrar/forms/TranscriptKey.jpg. Ask the students to read it over with the person sitting next to them and decide what the key terminology such as *GPA* and *rank* means. Confirm or correct the students suggestions in a whole-class discussion to round off the activity.

1 f, 2 c, 3 e, 4 a, 5 d, 6 b

**3** Refresh the students' memories about collocations and why it is worth learning them. Ask if anyone can explain the concept and be prepared to help with a definition.

Suggestion for a definition:
Words in English are often used in frequent partnership with other words. These word combinations are called collocations. In this exercise the focus is on adjective/noun collocations but other sorts of collocations are possible, for instance, between verbs and nouns. Collocations are worth learning as they enable learners of English to sound more natural.

Ensure that the students understand that collocations refer to word partnerships that one would expect to encounter frequently. They should also understand that one of the nouns in the list on the right is a red herring thrown in to make matters trickier. Now allow the students a couple of minutes to identify the collocations before bringing the class back together.

negotiable deadlines     corporate office
customized letters     valuable skills

**4** Your students should work on their own for listening exercises 4, 5 and 6. Before playing the CD for exercise 4, ask your students to read the points in the left-hand column of the table. Note they are to listen only for the answers to these questions and to disregard elements of the listening that they don't understand.

While they are listening, quickly draw the table on the board – to save time, you may want to prepare a slide with the table before class. After listening to the track elicit answers from your students and confirm the correct answers in the table you have drawn.

|  | Marc | Jennifer | Marion | Brian | Simon |
|---|---|---|---|---|---|
| Found his/her internship online | ✓ |  |  |  |  |
| Found his/her internship through connections |  | ✓ |  | ✓ |  |
| Created his/her own internship |  |  | ✓ |  | ✓ |
| Was paid for the internship | ✓ |  |  |  |  |
| Received no compensation for the internship |  |  |  | ✓ | ✓ |
| Speaker provides no information about pay |  | ✓ | ✓ |  |  |
| Talks about his/her job interview |  |  |  | ✓ | ✓ |

13

# 1 Applying for an internship

**5** Tell your students that they should now listen for specific words relevant in the context of student applications and that they will have to pay quite close attention to what is said. Assist students who have difficulty with this by pausing at the end of each Course Book sentence, thus giving students a chance to write the answers.

Collect answers by getting students to call these sentences out. Confirm that your students can spell the vocabulary focussed on by inviting those that volunteer answers to quickly come to the board and write the correct words.

**Marc**

1 I'm <u>majoring</u> in accounting and so I began <u>researching</u> on a number of websites in that field.
2 I was about to give up my <u>search</u> when I found the perfect <u>internship</u>, It even <u>paid a small salary</u> and included housing.
3 I <u>filled out</u> the application and was going to <u>submit</u> it <u>with a resumé</u> I had on my computer.

**Jennifer**

4 I <u>graduated</u> from Lake County Community College in May with a <u>degree in</u> Office Management.
5 One week later I found myself sitting in the <u>corporate office</u> of booksonline.com meeting with Shirley - my <u>potential supervisor</u>.

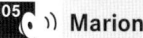

**Marion**

6 Then I <u>wrote customized letters</u> to six of them, stressing my personal qualities - you know, <u>conscientiousness, enthusiasm, resourcefulness</u>.
7 I can only recommend using your own imagination and creativity. It is one way around the <u>fierce competition</u> and really <u>makes a good impression</u>.

**6** Before playing the listening again, ask the students if they can recall what Brian and Simon said. Don't confirm the answers at this stage but play track 06 so that students can check themselves. You could also up the ante of this final listen through by asking which two collocations from stage 3 are used in the listening.

- Brian felt the recruitment process to be stressful because of the personal nature of the questions he was asked. For Simon the screening process was tough because of the questions about his skills in English that he had to answer.
- *Corporate office* and *customized letters* are featured in the listening.

**7** Get your students into pairs to discuss these questions. Tell them that their task is to come up with two lists which are as long as possible. A special task awaits the pair with the longest lists.

Collect the students' ideas in open class by writing them in two columns on the board. Allow some minutes for students to comment on each others' ideas. Some students may want to cite the exploitation of a cheap labor force as grounds for companies running internship programs. You might let discussion on this topic run longer. However, if you are short of time, cut this aspect of the discussion in order to have discussion time for the other factors.

1 **Answers may include:**
- increasing levels of work experience in general
- getting insight into a specific type of job
- increasing chances of getting a full-time job with a specific company, in a particular country or in a specific area after university
- gaining work experience in another country, and developing skills in a foreign language.

2 Interns are a useful and cost-effective supplement to existing work teams for companies. Running internship programs also offers companies the chance to get to know young professionals who they may later offer permanent employment to. Also, the PR boon that a company gets by offering internships to young people should not be forgotten.

Now ask your students to spend a few minutes studying the language box at the bottom right of the page. While they are doing so, brief your two "winners" as to their special tasks. Having studied the British English expressions and their American English equivalents, the other pairs will close their books. The winning pair's task is to ask the other students if they remember the equivalent expressions from the box: one student should ask for American equivalents to the British English expressions while the other asks for British equivalents to the American expressions. Ask the students to keep the pace quite high. This short but effective vocabulary drill will ensure that students learn this important vocabulary on the spot.

Make the best use of valuable classroom time by not asking students to write cover letters and resumés in class. Extra practice on both these aspects of writing applications is included in the *Over to you* section at the end of the unit.

14

# Applying for an internship 1

## Reading: **Recruiters' pet peeves**

**1** Divide your students into groups of four by putting pairs together. Teach *pet peeves* by offering a couple of examples of your own, such as *My biggest pet peeve is when students come late to my classes – I really hate that* and *Another pet peeve of mine is when people jump ahead of me in line*. Check your students understand the expression by asking them for a few similar examples.

Read the instructions with your class and ensure that the students know what to do by asking for volunteers to call out two or three ideas about the criteria that recruiters might use to sort applications. For example, they might "deselect" applications on the basis that they are too long, poorly spelt or incomplete.

Give the groups five minutes to come up with as long a list as possible of the criteria that recruiters might use.

**2** Tell the students that they are now going to read an article to see if the criteria that they thought of are referred to and if any additional criteria are mentioned. You might consider splitting this reading up within the group. Ask two students to read from the beginning to line 33 and the other two to read from line 34 to the end. Ask them to underline vocabulary or expressions they don't understand, but then to move on with their reading and attempt to understand the text without worrying about these words.

After reading the text invite the students to explain to each other what the half of the article they didn't read might contain. Their aim should be to draw up a list of the recruiters' criteria for comparison with their own lists.

 Criteria mentioned in the article are:
- **Negative criteria**: spelling errors, typos, poor grammar and layout on the page, poorly organized or irrelevant information and standardized resumés
- **Positive criteria**: tailored resumés, original supplementary material, perseverance

Round up this phase by writing *The dos and don't's of job applications* on the board and collaborating with the class to reformulate the information from the article into a useful checklist which they could use when writing applications:
*do – customize applications for each job you apply for*
*don't – send off a resumé you've used before and designed for another job.*

Now invite questions about vocabulary and expressions that students might not have understood. Expect to deal with the terms *process of elimination, confess* and *to use something with discretion*. Before providing your own explanations, ask if any other students can explain the words and expressions.

## Discussion: **Making your resumé stand out**

 Divide your students into new groups and set them the task of discussing and answering the three questions. Regarding the first of these three, focus their thinking by telling them that, in the light of the *dos* and *don't's* lists they have compiled, it is taken as granted that their applications won't contain typos or clumsy formatting. But what further positive steps could they take to ensure that proper attention is paid to their applications and not put in *File 13* (a trash can)? Be aware that you may be regarded by your students as an expert in matters of writing applications and spend some time before the class thinking about the advice you could offer, particularly with regard to how to supplement the traditional cover letter and resumé with other media. Before the groups attempt the third question, ensure that the words *franchisee* and *NGO* (*Non-governmental organization*, i.e. *Amnesty International*) are understood.

Round off by inviting a whole-class discussion during which groups can compare their answers.

1 be proactive, e.g. by calling a prospective employer, collecting information about the employer, asking a native speaker to check your application
2 video, project portfolio, link to your own website
3 **Advertising agency:** application should show creativity in the form of logos, layouts or advertising copy that applicants have produced
**Bank manager:** application should show good communication skills and the capability to deal with figures as well as an awareness of the correct financial terminology and current developments in the financial sector
**Fast food chain:** as well as detailed experience in catering, applicants should display team management and business experience
**NGO:** NGOs would expect a sincere interest in the issues they deal with, e.g. the environment, Third World, etc.

# 1 Applying for an internship

**Business Skills**

## Applications: Drafting your resumé

**1** Before your students get down to work on the questions, ask them to skim the resumé on their own with the aim of commenting about its structure, what sections is it organized into and what information is contained in each. Set a time limit of two minutes for this stage, then get students to call out their suggestions.

> **Personal data:** includes key personal information about the candidate as well as their contact information. Point out that this section can also be called *Personal details*.
>
> **Education:** contains an outline of the candidate's educational history.
>
> **Training:** includes details of training received by the candidate. The section also refers to a temporary job. Point out to your class that this could also be put under another section called *Employment* or *Work experience*.
>
> **Other experience:** details experiences gained outside work which the candidate feels are nevertheless of interest to the potential employer.
>
> **Special skills:** used to highlight skills which perhaps have not already been alluded to and which the candidate wants to draw particular attention to.
>
> **Interests:** gives a brief overview of what the candidate does in their spare time.

Point out that while Simon writes that he will provide references on request, it is standard to include a section called *References* or *Referees* in British CVs, which consists of the contact details of two people in a position to comment on the candidate. The first of these will usually be the current or last employer, though the referee could also be a university lecturer.

Now set your students the task of considering if Simon has written and laid out his resumé in accordance with the criteria already mentioned in class. Having read over the resumé, students should work with the person next to them to compare their answers. Set a three-minute time limit for this task, then finish off with an open discussion inviting a few volunteers to summarize their thoughts about Simon's resumé. Be sure to point out to students that an English resumé should not be dated and signed. It might also be worth pointing out that there is more than one type of resumé in the English-speaking world. Another type is the skills resumé in which the main focus is on the applicant's skills and education. Drawing attention to this point would also enable an elegant transition to the action verbs on the next page, which students might not be familiar with.

1 Answer depends on what has been mentioned in class. Simon's resumé is well organized and well formatted. It is easy to read because his job descriptions are seldom longer than one sentence. Wherever possible, he has used bullet points.
There is little customization in his resumé.

**2** Before students individually tackle the questions here, make sure that they understand the term *unique selling proposition*: USPs are aspects of a candidate's skills and experience which make them of particular interest to an employer over and above other candidates.

> Simon's USPs:
> He has a good general knowledge of business operations, as he has worked in a variety of departments. He appears to have good computer and IT skills (cf. setting up database). Since he is an assistant to the accounting professor, he is likely to have good math skills. His English appears to be fluent because he spent a year at high school in the U.S. His work at the summer camp and in community service suggests that he is good at dealing with people (social skills).
>
> Skills and experience
> - has some knowledge of American culture
> - is familiar with the work of special departments so can work independently
> - can take on responsibility
> - has very good English skills

Given time constraints, it would be advisable to avoid the temptation of having your students write their own resumés in class. The *Over to you* section of this unit will give students the opportunity to write their resumés, as well as cover letters, in English.

**3** Begin here by reminding students of the collocation task they carried out in exercise 3 on page 7. Point out to them that this exercise works along the same lines though, on this occasion, it is verb/noun collocations which are the focus.

You may choose to carry out this step and step 4 as homework. Motivate students to do this by underlining the usefulness of the language they are about to work on. It will allow them to sound more natural and "native speaker-like" in any applications they may write. Advise your students to refer to their dictionaries for definitions of some of the verbs. The phrasal verbs may be especially challenging.

**Applying for an internship** 1

Explain to your students that they can use a search engine on the internet to research whether particular word combinations occur frequently in written English. They should type a word combination in quotation marks which they want to examine into the search engine. This will prompt the search engine to find instances of the words used as an exact phrase. The results of their search will offer them some indication of how frequent a particular combination is and, therefore, if it is worth learning the collocation. Students may also check collocations at online collocation finders, such as http://www.natcorp.ox.ac.uk.

🔑
| deal with | customers |
| take care of | |
| handle | campaigns |
| analyze | statistics |
| compile | |

| carry out | a plan |
| implement | |
| improve | a database |
| manage | day-to-day office work |
| operate | machinery |
| participate in | research |
| | decision-making |
| prepare | presentations |
| research | reports |
| set up | a database |
| | campaigns |

**4** Based on their results in exercise 3, the students should also write their five sentences for homework. Students can send it to you for corrections and suggestions.

## Applications: **Drafting a cover letter**

**1** Refer your students back to the advertisement for internships at *American Fields* on page 6. Working in pairs, they have five minutes to make a list of *American Fields'* requirements. Get the students to say and write them on the board.

Now give the pairs a further ten minutes to read Simon's cover letter, so they can decide if his skills and experience meet the job requirements. When they have finished, invite two or three pairs to present their findings. This done, ask other students to say whether they disagree with the pairs and, if so, why.

🔑
- Simon feels *American Fields* is a good opportunity because of his personal background
- doesn't explicitly refer in his letter to his team skills and experience in analyzing data, but this is mentioned in his resumé
- refers to his interest in the food sector
- refers to his thorough training
- points out his foreign language skills, which are a prerequisite for working in the U.S.

**2** Ask your students to read the titles of the four main sections of a cover letter and decide quickly in their pairs the order in which Simon deals with these sections in his letter.

🔑
A Reference and reason for application
B USP (= unique selling proposition) or what makes him special
C Background
D Further steps

**3** Make sure that each pair has a dictionary at hand. Instruct your students to refer to their dictionaries only as a last resort when dealing with any unknown adjectives. Before the class attempts to do the exercise, ask if anyone can provide an explanation of *to think outside the box*.

🔑
- to think creatively without being hampered by conventional constraints

Introduce an element of fun and competition into the exercise in the following way. Tell the students that they are going to race to see who can complete the table correctly first. When the first pair put up their hands to indicate that they are finished, stop the other students and scan the pair's work for errors. If there aren't any, they win. If they get it wrong, tell them which adjectives they have sorted incorrectly but not where they really belong. Now return to the race. The first pair must hurry to correct their mistakes before other pairs finish ahead of them. When a pair finally presents a successfully completed table, stop the race, declare the winner and write the right answers on the board. You may wish to extend the activity at this point by introducing a second stage to the competition. Give the students a further three or four minutes to write in any other appropriate adjectives they can think of. The pair to make the greatest number of appropriate additions to the table wins.

# 1 Applying for an internship

| How to say that | Adjectives |
|---|---|
| you have objectives | ambitious, determined, motivated |
| you are good at what you do | conscientious, methodical, well-organized, reliable, good with numbers, analytical |
| you are good with people | communicative, adaptable, flexible, inspiring |
| you like getting things done | active, dynamic, decisive |
| you think outside the box | creative, critical, innovative |

**4** Your students should work on their own to write their five sentences. Remind them to use as many of the adjectives from exercise 3 as possible. While the pairs are discussing the sentences, move around the room and take a look at as many of the students' sentences as possible, taking note of any particular mistakes which you would like to draw attention to. Once the discussion is over, write the mistakes on the board and invite students to offer their own corrections.

There is no need to have your students write a cover letter at this stage. They will be given the opportunity to do so in the *Over to you* section at the end of the unit.

### Sentence Auction

1 Pre-teach *auction* by referring to *ebay* or other well-known examples of auctions.

2 Divide your students into pairs or small groups and explain that each sentence contains one mistake. The mistakes are either lexical (an incorrect expression is used) or grammatical in nature. Ask them to work together to correct the mistakes in the sentences. Do not correct your students at this stage.

3 Explain the rules of the auction. Each pair or group has a total of $1,500 to spend. Their goal is to buy as many correct sentences as possible by bidding in increments of $50 or $100. The students should keep a note of how much they have spent in the right-hand column of their worksheet.

4 Carry out the auction until all the sentences have been sold.

5 As a class, go over the sentences. Ask the groups which won each sentence to write their correction on the board. If it is correct, they keep the sentence. If it is incorrect, they lose it. The group with the most sentences at the end wins.

I would like to apply …
I was born on 17 August 1985.
… I did …
I did …
… I am studying …
… to hearing from you.
I worked in the Marketing department …
I have studied …

## Role-play: **Selling yourself**

To get started here ask your students to spend a few moments thinking of what their ideal internship would be. It is important that each student focuses their video presentation on a job they are interested in and equipped for in terms of their skills and experience. Once you are sure that all members of the class have something in mind, draw the students' attention to the phrases on the left of the page. Tell them that their aim is to use at least three of these phrases during their presentation.

Now spend a few minutes talking about the structure of the presentation and eliciting suggestions from students. Though other structures would be possible, remind the class of the cover letter on page 11, pointing out that its structure would provide an effective framework for the presentation.

Now give your students time to work on their own to prepare their presentations. Tell them that their aim should be to use all the time available pointing out that three minutes is not as long as it might sound, especially if they pace their delivery well and don't rush. Allow around 15 minutes for preparation during which you should be on hand to offer assistance with specific formulations. Point out that the students should avoid reading their presentations at all costs. To help them, they should not write them out in full but rather sketch them in note form. When they have finished, they should spend a few minutes silently practising the presentation.

You may want your students to video each others' presentations. If some students have digital cameras and laptops, ask them to bring them to the lesson. Form groups which include the students who have brought these items. Encourage students to listen actively to each other during the presentations. While they are listening have them take notes on structure, pace and presentation style. Listen in on as many presentations as possible so that you can identify two or three students whose presentations you find particularly successful.

After recording the presentation ask the students to transfer the videos onto the laptops. The students should now watch the presentations in their groups. At the end of each, students should summarize their comments, "rewind" to the appropriate part of a presentation where necessary in order to illustrate a particular point.

# Applying for an internship 1

Congratulate your students on their performance and discuss what made each presentation successful.

 **Video: An internship abroad: Interview**

Reinforce what your students have achieved through their presentations by using the first video clip. Warm the students up for this by asking them to brainstorm all the things they would do before going for an interview. Split the video into two parts: the interview itself and the scene where Harold enters the room.

Before playing the first scene, ask your students to think about preparing for an interview. What should Rebecca do to prepare for her interview? Also ask them what should Rebecca do if she forgets the words she learned for the interview, or if she is asked an unpredictable question.

Play the scene up to the point before Harold enters the room. Then ask your students to discuss and compare their impressions of Rebecca's performance with the person sitting next to them. Ask them what preparation she made. (She has researched the company, knows why she wants the job, and knows her strengths and weaknesses. Also Rebecca has ensured that her appearance is appropriate for the interview.)

Finally, ask the students to speculate about whether Rebecca will get the internship. Now play the closing scene after which you should ask the students to say whether they concur with Ms Robinson's assessment of Rebecca's performance.

## Company Case: **A challenging internship**

 Split your students into groups of three or four. Tell them to read about Sabine's experience of doing an internship in India. Ask the groups to quickly brainstorm what difficulties a student from a different culture might encounter during an internship in India. Bring the class back together to collect ideas. Ask the students to read the text to find out if any of the difficulties which they thought of are mentioned. When they are finished reading, ask a student to summarize the text.

Now allow your students to discuss and answer the questions in their groups. Allow a maximum of ten minutes for this before bringing the students back together for a whole-class discussion of the issues.

1. It was not necessarily naive of Sabine to choose to do her internship in India as her willingness to do so displays an adventurous spirit and the ability to think outside the box, which may be attractive to employers. Moreover, many people who spend a period of time living and working in a culture different to their own experience homesickness and disorientation at some stage. Sabine may well readjust to her setting and enjoy her internship again after a short time.
2. The change in her mood may be accounted for by homesickness, loneliness, "culture shock" and tiredness.
3. It may have been possible for her to research the experience she was about to have more thoroughly. This may have better prepared her: to accept her current feelings as a natural experience at some stage.
4. She should certainly now seek out the company of other people from her country in her city. Talking with them will probably act as a safety valve for her feelings. She should also make sure that her employers understand how she feels. They appear to be friendly and might be able to offer her additional support.

Ask your students to brainstorm ideas and draft the flyer in their groups within a ten-minute time frame. While they are doing so, monitor their work and be on hand to help with any formulations. When they are finished, they should hang their flyers on the classroom wall. Invite the students to look at each other's flyers and comment on each one.

Round off by recapping in discussion the problems that might potentially be faced by people doing internships in foreign cultures and possible solutions that might mitigate these problems. Could your students imagine doing an internship in a far-away country? Have they planned any internships in the near future?

# 1 Applying for an internship

## Over to you

### Research yourself: SWOT analysis

Encourage your students to complete the SWOT analysis by telling them that they will do this task in the next lesson. They should email their analyses to you in advance. Select points written under each category by several students and copy them into a word document. Leave sufficient space between each point so that you can cut the paper into strips containing one point each.

During the next lesson, split your students into groups giving each group a set of cut-up strips. The students' task is to arrange these strips according to the appropriate categories. Round off by asking a few students to say which points mentioned apply to them and if there might be any other points they would like to add.

### Web research: Job opportunities on the net

Your students may find the following websites a useful starting point in their search for internships:

http://www.goabroad.com/

http://www.projects-abroad.org

At the start of the next lesson, give each student who has brought an advertisement one minute to say why they are interested in the internship and how their particular skills and experience equip them for it. Be sure to bring a few spare advertisements that you have selected yourself and give them to any students who have come unprepared.

### Writing: Drafting your resumé

Emphasize the importance of this exercise and offer to take a detailed look at their resumés. Given their importance, the resumés could be considered "work in progress".

### Writing: Composing a cover letter

Encourage your students to complete this task by offering to comment in detail on their letters. Advise them to look again at the letter on page 11 and point out that, though cover letters should be customized to each job applied for with respect to how skills and experience are presented much of the language of such letters is standardized. Invite students to identify as many standard, "framework" sentences as possible in this letter and to use these sentences in their own resumés.

# 2

# Work and p(l)ay

## At a glance

This unit's examination of jobs and careers will bring home to students the direct relevance of their English course which will help to equip them for the career of their choice.

The unit begins by considering the range of factors which affect career choice ranging from **salary**, opportunities for **promotion** and **work-life balance** to **job security** and **fringe benefits**. The latter is considered in the context of the **perks** on offer to staff at mould-breaking employers such as *Google* and *Boston Consulting Group*. Students will also come across other key vocabulary related to jobs and work including **staff turnover, remediation, redundancy** and **dismissal**.

The unit's *Business Skills* section focuses on email communication and acquaints students with a packed toolbox of key functional phrases for writing business emails, as well as encouraging them to consider the appropriateness of different writing tones ranging between the formal and informal. The *Company Case* takes into account the intercultural tensions faced by businesses when confronted with different attitudes to **work, pay** and **remuneration** in other countries.

For an overview of the legislation and regulations which shape employment practices in the E.U. see:
http://ec.europa.eu/social/ and click on *English*.

For concise information about the management issues touched upon in the unit see:
http://managementhelp.org/hr_mgmnt/hr_mgmnt.htm

## Warm-up

Ensure that your students understand the term *fringe benefits* and give them a few minutes to rank the factors in the list, pointing out that they can add any points not already mentioned which occur to them. Bring the class back together and ask if anyone thought of other factors which could be added to the list and write these on the board. Allow a couple of minutes for discussion.

### Self Study

**Vocabulary**
- A nice place to work
- Word families
- Finding the other half: Statements on work and pay

**Grammar**
- Tense practice: The simple present and present continuous
- Using the apostrophe
- Forming questions: Asking about working conditions

**Skills**
- Writing an email to reschedule a meeting
- Formal and informal style in emails I: Formal
- Formal and informal style in emails II: Informal
- Agreeing and disagreeing

**Reading**
- Recognizing paraphrased ideas
- In other words: Recognizing paraphrased statements

## Reading: **Best places to work**

**1** Complete this first task as a whole-class brainstorming and discussion activity. If nobody has heard anything concrete about working conditions at *Google*, ask the students to speculate as to what type of working conditions might be on offer in a modern internet company of this sort. If there are only a few answers, go on to ask what they would expect or hope from an ideal employer. Write their suggestions on the board.

**2** Ask your students to read the first part of the text swiftly looking for the benefits which are on offer. When they have finished reading, ask two or three people to compare their speculations with what the article says. Ask a few other students to comment on which of the benefits surprised them and why.

**3** Your students should now read over the true/false questions about *Boston Consulting Group* and bear these in mind when scan reading the remainder of the article. Students should ignore vocabulary they don't understand in the meantime. Check answers in open class.

🔑 1 **true**, 2 **true**, 3 **false**, 4 **true**, 5 **false**

# 2 Work and p(l)ay

**4** Point out to students that they should scan read the text again for the purposes of this exercise. Once they have done so, get two or three students to call out the benefits they have identified. You might decide to throw in an aside about another benefit of working for *Google* not mentioned in the text. Development engineers at the company get to spend 20% of their time working on projects which are not part of their job description, a policy designed to boost innovation and employee satisfaction.

| Google: | Boston Consulting Group: | Other benefits mentioned: |
|---|---|---|
| • on-site pool<br>• gourmet restaurants<br>• climbing wall<br>• unlimited sick leave<br>• five weeks' paid time off<br>• tuition reimbursement<br>• classes in foreign languages | • independence in deciding on career path<br>• professional development<br>• counseling<br>• maternity leave<br>• benefits to spouses and domestic partners<br>• emergency child care | • paternity leave<br>• flexible working schedule |

**5** Tell students that they will now get the chance to read the text in more detail. You may extend the communicative scope of the exercise by asking students to discuss potential answers with the person sitting next to them. In any case, allow ten minutes for reading before bringing the class back together.

- to reply to a question with *yes*
  **to answer in the affirmative**
- the form one's professional life will take
  **the shape and trajectory of their career**
- a person responsible for young employees who will listen to their problems
  **office sponsor with a non-evaluative role**
- firms not included in the ranking
  **companies who don't make the list**
- the person to whom you are married
  **spouse**
- to adapt the work schedule to an employee's individual needs
  **to customize the program to make it easy for employees to deal with their lives**

At this stage you can invite questions about vocabulary from the article which the students weren't familiar with. Be prepared to assist them to understand the terms *reimbursement*, *affirmative*, *resumé*, *topical*, *trajectory*, *maternity* and *paternity leave*.

## Discussion: What matters in a job?

**1** Put your students into pairs, ensure they understand *window dressing* and ask them to discuss the questions. Allow around five minutes for this then bring the class back together to collect answers.

**2** Now form groups by putting pairs together and ask the students to spend a minute making a list of their personal *must-haves*. Students should then discuss their *must-haves* with the other students in the group discussing why they are important to them personally. Listen in to the discussions in order to identify two or three students who have contrasting priorities. At the end, bring the class back together and ask these students to go through their *must-haves* and explain their choices.

**3** Ask the groups to discuss the reasons which lie behind some companies' "generosity" to employees before collecting and discussing the students' suggestions in open class.

# Work and p(l)ay 2

## Listening: Talking about professional life

**1** Give your students four or five minutes to complete the gap-fill before bringing the class back together to check answers. Encourage students to refer to their dictionaries to find definitions of any terms they are unsure of.

1 His failure to come to work on time was the reason for his <u>dismissal</u>.
2 His plans for <u>retirement</u> include buying a yacht and sailing around the world.
3 I have an <u>expense account</u> of $20,000 a year and spend most of it on entertaining clients.
4 If the company outsources its production to Southeast Asia, there are sure to be a lot of <u>redundancies</u>.
5 If your employer is not satisfied with your work during your <u>probationary period</u>, you won't be given a permanent contract.
6 The workers who had been laid off were offered some financial <u>compensation</u>.
7 Modern technology has provided solutions for the speedy <u>remediation</u> of contaminated industrial sites.

**2** Tell your students that this exercise will acquaint them with some key idiomatic expressions used in the listening and ask them to work with the person sitting next to them to complete the matching. Check answers in open class.

1 c, 2 d, 3 a, 4 b

**3** Ask your students to read the seven statements and bear these in mind when listening. After you have played the listening, confirm the answers in open class.

1 **true**, 2 **true**, 3 **false**, 4 **false**, 5 **false**, 6 **true**, 7 **true**

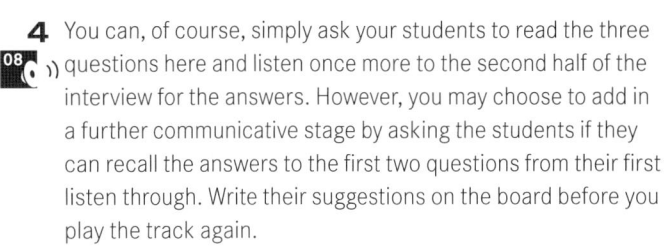

**4** You can, of course, simply ask your students to read the three questions here and listen once more to the second half of the interview for the answers. However, you may choose to add in a further communicative stage by asking the students if they can recall the answers to the first two questions from their first listen through. Write their suggestions on the board before you play the track again.

You could then ask students to work with the person sitting next to them to come up with a collaborative answer to the third question. Discuss the ideas in open class.

1 **Joanna**
 • manages the office
 • does the bookkeeping
 • takes care of the PR
 • coordinates the activities of team members
 • plans meetings
 • designs presentations
 • makes travel arrangements
 • accompanies her boss to construction sites

2 **The environmental consultancy**
 • makes sure companies comply with official environmental standards
 • advises companies on remediation projects
 • deals with routine waste management

3 **Global market**
 • Environmental awareness has increased so governments make sure that companies comply with regulations and standards.
 • The E.U. has developed environmental guidelines which have to be followed by its member states.
 • The U.K. has a lot of derelict land formerly occupied by heavy industries. If this land is to be reused, developers have to make sure that hidden environmental hazards are detected and cleaned up.

## Role-play: How to make good people stay

### So, can we agree to that?

This activity can be used as preparation for the role-play and provides additional functional phrases which can be integrated into the role-play.

Split your students into pairs giving each pair a set of cut-up and shuffled cards. Allow the students three minutes to cloze the phrases on the cards. While they are doing this, write the functional categories of the phrases on the board: *Suggesting*, *Looking for agreement*, *Rejecting a suggestion*, *Asking for clarification* and *Rounding up*.

Next, check quickly that the students have matched the cards correctly by getting them to call out the phrases they have formed, then give the pairs another three minutes to decide which functional heading they would put each phrase under. Again, check answers in open class.

The role-play can now be carried out by the pairs with the cards spread in front of them. Their task is to complete the role-play using as many of the phrases as possible. The first student to use a phrase gets a point; the next can use the phrase again but doesn't receive a point for it. The student with the most points at the end wins.

# 2 Work and p(l)ay

**Business Skills**

## Email writing: Sending the right message

1 Split your students into pairs to address the questions. After allowing up to five minutes for discussion, bring the class back together and ask a few students to describe their personal preferences. Extend the discussion by asking if they can think of particular subjects which are more appropriately dealt with face-to-face or in writing and which type of subjects would almost certainly not be discussed using text messaging.

2 It may be necessary to prompt students' thinking here as some of them may have little experience to base their ideas on. You could use ideas from the following link, http://www.emailreplies.com/

After a few minutes bring the students back together collecting their ideas on the board. Round off by collaborating with the class to write up a check list of *do's* about writing business emails which students should record in their notebooks.

3 Set the students the task of describing the functions of the highlighted phrases, then collect answers in open class. Don't forget to explain that, as such phrases are used repeatedly and almost unaltered in emails, being able to identify, learn and use them is a worthwhile enterprise.

Now ask the pairs to work on the other emails. Point out that, along with containing phrases which fulfill the functions already identified by students in email 4, the other emails contain phrases which fulfill other functions.

Allow the students up to ten minutes to explore the emails before bringing the class back together to check results. You may choose to do this by coming to class armed with the three emails on slides for projection and asking three pairs to come one at a time to the front of the class to highlight phrases – and describe the function of these – in one of the emails. The other students should be invited to make their own comments. Be prepared to intervene and assist students in their description of the functions.

4 As the students have already read the emails, this task can be carried out relatively swiftly. Allow the pairs two or three minutes to scan read the emails and decide which is which before confirming the correct answers.

> A an arrangement of an appointment
> B an attempt to inform
> C an enquiry
> D a request for action

5 Allow the students up to ten minutes to consider these questions before discussing them in open class. Advise your students to add the points they arrive at about the importance of clear structure to the list of "do's" they created collaboratively in exercise 2.

6 Your students now get the opportunity to sort the functional language they have identified in the emails under the appropriate headings. Collect answers by asking individual students to explain which phrases they have included under a particular heading until all of the phrases have been dealt with.

|  | Formal style | Informal style |
| --- | --- | --- |
| Greeting | Dear Sir or Madam<br>Dear Ms (last name) | Hello (first name)<br>(first name) |
| Opening/References | With reference to …<br>Thank you very much for … | You will be glad to hear … |
| Request | Please contact us as soon as possible to confirm this date. | Can you do some research …? |
| Enquiry | I am writing to enquire about … |  |
| Arrangements | We would like to invite you …<br>Please let me know if this date is convenient for you. | How about meeting … |
| Attachments | Please find all the relevant details in my attached CV. | I'm attaching … |
| Giving good news | We are very pleased to inform you … | We are happy to tell you that … |
| Polite ending | I am looking forward to hearing from you soon.<br>Please contact us if we can be of service to you. | Thanks a lot.<br>Hope to hear from you soon. |
| Closing | Yours sincerely<br>Yours faithfully | Cheers<br>All the best |

# Work and p(l)ay 2

## Email writing: Getting the answer right

Split your students into new pairs to complete this exercise. Should you decide that your students will require some support in completing it, tell them that they are looking for a change in style in two of the emails. Allow the pairs up to ten minutes for reading and discussion before bringing the class back together to confirm the correct answers. Be sure to allow sufficient time at this stage for the students to discuss the reasons which might lie behind these changes in style. Extend the scope of this discussion by asking students if they feel that the changes in style they have identified are justified.

### Email puzzle

Pair off your students giving each pair the two emails cut up into strips and thoroughly shuffled. Explain that their first task is to cloze the sentences from the emails. While they are doing so, circulate and check their progress giving hints where necessary. When the students have successfully completed this stage, clarify that they are dealing with two emails and that the pairs are to work together to sort the sentences into the appropriate email and then into a logical order within each email. Introduce an element of competition into the proceedings by explaining that the emails are from two of Joanna's correspondents from page 20 of the Course Book: the first pair to reassemble both emails successfully, then say who they are from, wins.

Email A – from Roy Ellis
Email B – from Jill Masters

## Writing: Finding the right style

You may consider setting the writing stage of the exercise as homework so as to save valuable classroom time. In any case, ask your students to refer back to the functional expressions which they have identified on pages 20 and 21 and to include as much of the phrases as is appropriate. If you have set the writing as homework, select three or four emails which you judge to be particularly successful and copy them onto slides for projection to enable discussion with the whole class. You should keep these anonymous in the first instance.

At the next class, re-form the pairs and ask students to swap their emails. Allow five minutes for reading and note-taking, then invite the students to comment upon each others work. Circulate and be on-hand to reinforce positive criticism offered by students.

When the discussion has run its course, project the emails you have selected asking the students to read over them quickly and comment on style and the use of functional phrases. Be sure to point out what you liked about these emails.

## Company Case: A clash of cultures

Tell your students that they are going to read about a clash of cultures between North American and East Asian attitudes to pay and work and ask them to consider the first two bullet points on the list inviting students to call out their suggestions about American and East Asian work culture. Should you have students of East Asian origin in your class, remember to draw upon their particular insight. Note the students' ideas on the board.

Now divide your students into small groups and ask them to read the text rapidly with the aim of finding out if any of the differences in culture which they suggested are alluded to or implied in the text. Quickly bring the class back together when the students have finished their scan reading and ask for comments about whether any of the students' suggestions about differences in culture can be squared with the case study. Be sure to encourage your students to explain their ideas in full. This will have the two-fold effect of testing and reinforcing their comprehension of the text and prompting critical thinking about it.

Next, invite the students to consider the three remaining bullet points in their groups. Remind them that they are going to report their observations to the class: they should make notes of what they decide during their discussion. Encourage students to make full use of *Conditional II* when preparing their answers to the final question.

Allow up to 15 minutes for discussions before bringing the class back together and inviting the groups to report their findings. Be sure to leave sufficient time at the end of this for further discussion relating to points raised by students.

25

# 2 Work and p(l)ay

## Over to you

### Skills: Softening feedback

Point out the particular importance of expressing direct messages in diplomatic and formal language and encourage your students to complete the exercise. Ask your students to send their sentences to you well in advance of the next lesson at which you should spend a few minutes discussing their efforts with them. Don't forget to hand back the students' work complete with your comments.

1. I'm afraid to tell you/We regret to inform you that your qualifications do not meet our requirements.
2. I don't want to sound unhelpful but/Unfortunately my workload at the moment leaves me no time to assist you in your project.
3. Could you check the figures again? It seems as if they are not quite right./I would appreciate it if you could double-check your figures, as there seems to be an error.
4. Ms Clark was wondering if you could meet her next Friday at 12 o'clock?
5. I'd like to inform you that the meeting was cancelled.
6. I'm very happy to inform you that the new product line has proved a great success.
7. Would the time be convenient for you?

### Reading: The blue-eyed salaryman

Encourage your students to do this exercise by pointing out that the text offers further insight into the intercultural differences in attitudes to work touched on in the case study.

**2**

1. the person who protects the company from theft
   **security guard**
2. to travel daily between your home and your place of work
   **to commute**
3. a residential area situated outside a city
   **a suburb**
4. a person who has just been hired by a company
   **recruit**
5. a little pin a person wears to show who s/he is
   **ID badge**
6. the department concerned with hiring (and firing) employees
   **personnel**
7. a statement in which you tell someone you are sorry for something
   **an apology**
8. a place where you can do a Master's degree or a PhD
   **graduate school**
9. material, substance (also: a set of unspecified objects)
   **stuff**

**3**
1. Students' answers will depend on the companies that they are familiar with.
2. 
   - He has done a lot of unusual things, e.g. he has been a sailor and hitchhiked through various countries.
   - He obviously never had a clear idea about his career path.
   - It was by pure coincidence that he ended up in Japan.
3. 
   - They are proud of their jobs (security guard) and do the work conscientiously.
   - The company seems to expect that newcomers have to learn at lot before they can do their job properly.

**4**

1. line 43 ff.
2. line 45 ff.
3. line 26 ff.
4. line 49 ff.
5. line 55 ff.
6. line 26 ff.
7. line 38 ff.

### Web research: Benefits

Ensure that each student has two companies to research by brainstorming a list of international companies with the class to supplement the suggestions in the Course Book. Encourage the students to structure their research notes in such a way that they can make a quick presentation of their findings at the next class.

# 3 Customer service

## At a glance

Customer service – or the lack of it – is something which most people have experience of. Taking this as its starting point, this unit of *Career Express Business English B2* provides repeated opportunity for you to engage your students' personal interest and get them to reflect on their experience. However, in the course of the unit students get to change their perspective, away from the consumer point of view to that of the business. As the unit progresses, students are given the chance to evaluate customer service delivered on the telephone and are asked to create guidelines for call center agents.

The unit will also equip students with the key lexis to discuss customer service including terms, such as **recoup**, **refund**, **voucher**, **warranty** and **replacement**. Additionally, the unit examines important functional language for **complaining**, **apologizing** and **empathizing** and introduces students to a communication model that can be used to ensure the quality of customer care on the telephone.

The unit's *Business Skills* section focuses on the delivery of customer service on the telephone. Students are given the opportunity to evaluate the effectiveness of this in a series of listening exercises before practising the language they have encountered in two realistic role-plays. In the case study about poor customer service in a department store chain, students wear the manager's hat and have to originate strategies for improving service. Further practice in delivering customer service by email is offered in the *Over to you* section.

For articles about the imperatives facing customer service professionals see:
http://www.customerservicemanager.com

This short article provides a quick overview of how businesses guarantee quality in call centers:
http://www.customerservicepoint.com/quality-call-center.html

### Self Study

**Vocabulary**
- Adjectives describing customer service
- Customer service verbalized
- Frequently used nouns in customer service

**Grammar**
- Tense practice: simple past – present perfect – past continuous
- Timewise: *for – since – ago*
- Get a grip on prepositions!

**Skills**
- Telephone phrases: saying the right thing
- Telephoning: anticipating the customer's needs
- Using modals to form polite questions

**Reading**
- Call logging: reading comprehension
- Guessing meaning from context

## Warm-up

Customer service – or rather, the lack of it – will be part of the daily experience of your students and you will easily be able to capture their interest as a result of this. Conduct the warm-up exercise with the whole class, prompting and eliciting answers. Attempt to keep the tone of this warm-up light-hearted and try to mobilize the almost comic, minor tragedy of many customer service experiences to ensure your students' participation.

Begin by asking your students to consider the cartoon. What might the cartoonist be saying about the theory and practice of customer service? Give students a moment to consider their answers. Ask a student to comment upon the cartoonist's intentions – there will probably be unanimous agreement that the cartoonist is illustrating the gulf between theory and practice which frequently occurs in customer service – and round off this stage by asking students for a show of hands as to whether they think the customer service they receive is, in general, satisfactory or unsatisfactory.

The chances are that at least a few of your students have experience of working as call center agents and know the service worker perspective. Ensure that you spend sufficient time, then, on the first question on the list to tap into their perspectives. Ask them what sort of experience of call center

27

# 3 Customer service

work they have had. What pressures are call center agents under that make delivering good customer service difficult? Which improvements could be made in working practices in call centers to ensure a better deal for customers? Also try to elicit from those students what the most frequently occurring problems experienced by customers are.

Finally, ask students to swap customer service "horror stories" with the person sitting next to them: listen in on their conversations, taking note of two or three particularly interesting stories. Finally, ask the students whose partners related these particular anecdotes to retell them for the other students: the original narrators can jump in to assist where necessary.

## Reading: Customers' complaints

**1** Give your students a minute or so to consider the words and phrases in the margin: tell them they should identify those terms which they feel they can explain in their own words. They should not read the sentences at this stage. When their time is up bring the students back together and go over each word or phrase asking for a volunteer to define it. Be prepared to nudge the explanations in the right direction where necessary.

When you are satisfied that the class has a good working understanding of the vocabulary, ask yours students to complete the sentences. Check answers in open class.

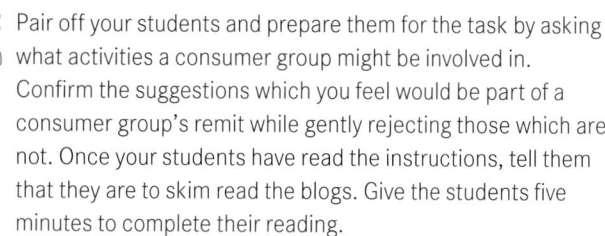

1. The company <u>overcharged</u> the customer.
2. According to the sales contract the customer <u>was entitled to</u> take advantage of special offers.
3. Although it was the customer's fault that the product stopped working, he was able to <u>recoup his money</u>.
4. The usual <u>warranty</u> for a product is six months.
5. There are three different ways a company can compensate a customer for a mistake: hand out a <u>voucher</u>, provide the customer with <u>a replacement</u> or give the customer <u>a refund</u>.

**2** Pair off your students and prepare them for the task by asking what activities a consumer group might be involved in. Confirm the suggestions which you feel would be part of a consumer group's remit while gently rejecting those which are not. Once your students have read the instructions, tell them that they are to skim read the blogs. Give the students five minutes to complete their reading.

Now bring the class back together, take each blog entry in turn and ask for comments as to what the reasons for the failures might have been. As there are no "right answers" here, be sure to allow plenty of time for students to make their suggestions and comment upon those of other students. Wind up the discussion of each entry by asking for a summary of what mistakes were made and note these on a sheet of paper. When all four blog entries have been dealt with, go over the list of mistakes that you have noted and ask the students to try to categorize the mistakes. Once the students agree on how to categorize a mistake, write it up on the board under that category heading.

**Possible ways of categorizing the mistakes:**
- **Lack of reliability and accuracy:** records are not kept correctly; the service is not performed right the first time
- **Lack of courtesy:** the company representative does not demonstrate politeness and respect for the customer
- **Lack of competence:** employees lack the knowledge and skills to deal with the customer's request
- **Lack of responsiveness:** employees fail to react promptly to a customer concern
- **Lack of accessibility:** the customer cannot reach company representatives
- **Failure to behave proactively:** the company does not anticipate customers' needs

**3** Form your students into four groups, assigning each one of the blog entries. Give the groups ten minutes to consider the questions: one student in each group should take note of the discussion to help them report back to the class at the end.

When the discussion phase is over, ask a volunteer from each group to present what the group decided: allow time for students from other groups to comment after each group report is delivered.

**4** Tell your students that you would like all of them to write a blog about a customer service catastrophe that they have experienced as homework.

Pair up your students for the exercise. The pair work element should work as follows: once students have finished writing their own blog entries, they should read their partners and then enter a comment empathizing with it and perhaps offering a similar experience of their own.

Be sure to read your students' blogs in advance of the next class and come to the lesson armed with your feedback for them.

# Customer service   3

## Listening: **LEARN**ing to listen

**1** Ask your students to close their Course Books, then write LEARN on the board. Explain that this is an acronym which describes a systematic model for dealing with customers on the phone: can they think of what the letters might stand for? Be prepared to prompt your students should they not be able to make appropriate suggestions. Once the class has established the words which make up the acronym, ask the students which phrases might be used by a call center agent at each stage of the LEARN concept. Write their suggestions on the board: for instance, for *Listen* this might include *I see*; *OK* and for *React*, *Right, I'm going to ...* ; *Let me tell you what I'll do to ...*, etc.

Now ask your students to open their Course Books and read the instructions. Before playing the listening, ensure that students understand their task: they are to listen only in order to establish if the call center agent adheres to the LEARN concept.

Discuss this in open class when the listening is over asking students to give reasons for their answers.

**Listen:** the customer service agent listens carefully for precise information, if she doesn't get any, she asks yes/no questions to get a more detailed idea about the problem (for example, when she realizes that *Volksbank* might be a foreign bank)
**Empathize:** *Don't worry, we call foreign banks every day.*
**Apologize:** *I'm afraid we have to verify all credit cards issued by a foreign bank.*
*I'm afraid you can't place your order until we've done that.*
**Notify:** *We should be able to verify your credit card within 24 hours at most. I suggest you call us back tomorrow.*

**2** Ask your students to read over the table to prepare themselves for the functions of the phrases they are to listen for. Now play the CD track again and collect answers in open class. Use the audioscript of the listening to provide gentle correction of wording in the event of students getting this wrong.

| Function | Agent | Customer |
|---|---|---|
| Starting a conversation | Good morning. (company name), (Doris) speaking. How can I help you? | |
| Stating the purpose of the call | | I've just been trying to ... |
| Checking information | Could you tell me what the problem seems to be? Is the shipping address outside the U.S.? Is that right? | |
| Apologizing | I'm very sorry but ... I'm afraid we have to ... / you can't ... | |
| Showing empathy | I understand that you're upset. | |
| Confirming information | Let me read this back to you: ... | |
| Spelling words | Could you spell this for me, please? | |
| Saying that you didn't understand | Sorry but I didn't get that. | What do you mean by that? |
| Assuring | Don't worry. | |
| Ending a conversation | Is there anything else I can do for you ...? Thank you for calling. | |

### Teleshopping

Use this photocopiable activity, which features key phrases from the preceding listening exercise, to prepare your students for the role-play which follows.

Split your students into pairs or small groups giving each pair or group a copy of the telephone dialog cut up as indicated. Instruct the students to shuffle the slips of paper thoroughly. Now tell them that each slip contains a separate utterance from a conversation on the phone between a call center agent and a customer. Their task is to reconstruct the dialog. If you feel that your students will manage this with little difficulty, turn it into a race: the first students to reassemble the dialog correctly are the winners.

# 3 Customer service

**3** Tell your students that they are to assume the roles of Frank Meier and the *Street Wise* customer service agent from track 09 and that they are to follow up on the phone call they have just listened to. Ask students to get into pairs and decide who will play A and B. Give them two to three minutes to read the email and their role cards, then ask your students to refer back to the phrases they encountered in exercise 2 and the photocopiable activity: they should select up to six of these phrases appropriate to their role and try to use them in the course of the role-play. Ask the pairs to sit back-to-back to carry out their telephone conversation.

**4** Quickly form small groups to address this question by putting pairs together. Get your students thinking critically here by putting additional questions to them: *In what ways might the LEARN concept be useful for call center workers? What might the limits of the concept be?* Give the groups five minutes to list the pros and cons of the LEARN concept as applied to the call center context. Bring the class back together asking students to volunteer their ideas: list these on the board. Make sure to come back to those students who have worked in call centers and ask them whether they think the LEARN concept would have been useful for them.

### Business Skills

## Telephoning: Evaluating telephone performance

**1** Ask your students to read the instructions, then check that they understand their task by asking a student to recap what they are to do in his/her own words. Don't forget to check that your students understand the scoring system. Now allow a couple of minutes for them to read over the nine points on the evaluation form and emphasize that they should bear these questions in mind when listening.

Pause the CD after each telephone conversation to give your students an opportunity to finish rating the call. Additionally, spend one or two minutes discussing their reactions to the call. Once you have played each of the CD tracks in turn, give your students a little time to reconsider how they have scored each call center agent: it may be the case that, having heard all three telephone conversations, students may wish to revise some of the scores.

Now bring the class back together and, taking each telephone conversation in turn, ask for volunteers to say how well the call center agent performed on each of the criteria. Students should say which score they awarded and back this up with evidence from the conversation. Allow plenty of time for other students to disagree with their classmates. Disagreement also has to be backed up with evidence from the conversations. Once the three conversations have been dealt with in this way, offer a verbal summary of what the students have said regarding each conversation.

The following rankings are to be regarded as suggestions. Students might well come up with other rankings. They should be able to explain their rankings.

|  | Conversation 1 | Conversation 2 | Conversation 3 | |
|---|---|---|---|---|
| Was the customer put through promptly to the right person? | 1 | 2 | 5 | 5 = excellent<br>4 = good<br>3 = satisfactory<br>2 = bad<br>1 = terrible |
| Does the representative give the customer her/his undivided attention? | 1 | 4 | 5 | |
| Does the person sound interested and concerned? | 2 | 3 | 5 | |
| Was the representative able to identify the problem quickly? | 1 | 3 | N.A. | |
| Did s/he appear knowledgeable? | 5 | 3 | N.A. | |
| Did the person avoid technical jargon and use language the customer could understand? | 2 | 3 | N.A. | |
| If the employee was unable to answer the customer's request, did s/he offer options or alternatives? | 1 | 1 | N.A. | |
| If an error had been made, did the employee apologize? | 1 | 1 | 5 | |
| Was the representative's telephone behavior courteous and professional? | 3 | 2 | 5 | |

30

# Customer service 3

 Telephone performance – A manager's evaluation

Use this activity to extend the listening exercise. Put your students into small groups giving each group the sentences cut up in strips as indicated. Ask them to shuffle the strips thoroughly. Now explain that the sentences are notes on two of the three phone conversations made by one of the managers who attended the seminar. The students should spread the strips out and work collaboratively to establish, which two conversations they refer to and, second, which notes refer to which conversation. Explain that three of the notes do not refer to either of the conversations. They are there to make matters more challenging; the students should identify these and weed them out. Get your students to do this in the first instance without listening to the three conversations again: the emphasis should be on them discussing their recollections of the conversations in order to sort the notes correctly.

When they have identified that the notes refer only to the first two conversations and have more or less completed assigning each note to the right conversation, play the two CD tracks again so that they can check the way they have sorted the notes. Allow a few more minutes for further group discussion, then bring the class back together to confirm the correct answers.

 **2** Divide your students into groups and give them ten minutes to discuss and draft their guidelines. Again, turn to those students who have worked in call centers before and ask them to bring in their experience to create truly helpful guidelines. Then bring the class back together and ask the different groups to present their guidelines. If the different groups come up with very divergent ideas, ask them to elaborate on the thinking behind their guidelines.

## Role-play: **Complaining and apologizing**

 Ask your students which of them are to take roles A and B, then give them some minutes to study the situation and their roles.

Now bring the As and Bs together in two groups at either end of the classroom. Quickly set the call center agents the task of revising the language they will require for the role-play which they encountered on page 28. While they are doing this, turn your attention to the irate customers and spend some time giving them language for expressing their annoyance: provide them with a few phrases which they can use to express their displeasure, such as *I'm really not amused by this* and *I don't think this is tolerable at all*.

Now split your students into pairs of As and Bs asking them to sit back-to-back for the purposes of the role-play. Encourage the students playing the customer to be as impolite and awkward as possible without being downright rude. During the course of this, listen in to as many conversations as possible in order to identify one or two pairs of students who do particularly well. When the students have finished role-playing, ask the students you have identified to carry out their role-play in front of the class: the other students are to take notes and comment upon their classmates' work.

## Diversity: **Consumers' refusal**

 Split your students into groups and feed them a piece of vocabulary which is used in various industries to denote the phenomenon detailed in the table: *customer churn*. Without encouraging students to carry out an exact analysis of the data, ask them to establish which countries tend to have higher churn levels than others before they discuss the reasons for this. Suggest to students that, while distinct expectations about customer service will undoubtedly play a role in creating different levels of churn between countries, other factors might also be at play. For instance, the maturity of the market for a particular service in a country may be decisive here. If competition is underdeveloped in a given sector and there are few alternative choices, customers will be more inclined to stay put despite unsatisfactory customer service. Ask students to brainstorm as many of these potential factors as possible. Allow the students up to 15 minutes to analyze the data and discuss its implications fully. Consolidate the activity by bringing the class back together and asking the groups to summarize the results of their discussion. Be sure to allow enough time for discussion in the event of disagreement between groups.

Round off the activity by asking a few volunteers to describe their own patterns of switching service providers and explaining the reasons for this.

You may wish your students to remain in the same groups for the next exercise.

31

# 3 Customer service

## Company Case: **Service desert?**

Draw your students' attention to the title of the case study. Ask them if they think that customer service is particularly bad in their country. Can they offer any stories from other countries about poor customer service? Spend two or three minutes on this.

Now turn your students' attention to the text and give them a maximum of three minutes to skim read it, so that they can briefly summarize its contents. Then call upon two or three students to provide a summary for the rest of the class.

Your students should now work in small groups to consider the questions and design an action plan which Lehmann could use to improve customer service in his stores. Encourage your students to present their ideas in a clear presentation format including an introduction, a main body of argument, a summary and a conclusion.

Now bring the class back together and ask volunteers from each group to present their action plans. Allow enough time at the end of each presentation for other students' comments. As students deliver their presentations, summarize their suggestions on the board using key words such as *increase staff training* or *introduce customer service mentoring system*. Use this as an opportunity to reformulate students' suggestions should this be necessary. Once all the presentations have been given, turn to what you have written on the board and ask students to decide what they personally feel would be the three most effective and important measures. Tally up the results.

Finally, round off the activity with a whole-class discussion about why customer service can be lacking and why customers tolerate this.

# Over to you

## Field research: Customer satisfaction

Encourage students to carry out this exercise by setting a clearly structured task. Split the class into several research groups each of which you should give a specific service point to investigate: the university cafeteria, the public transport service to the university, the university's student administration offices. Each group is to develop a questionnaire which is specific to the service point they are to carry out. Collate their research before the next class. Clearly, the survey will have to be carried out in the students' own language and the results translated into English for the purposes of discussion in class. At the next class, give each group the opportunity to report what it found out.

## Email practice: Complaining and apologizing politely

Students should send the emails to each other as well as to you. Select the most successful or interesting ones and show them to the class anonymously with your comments and corrections.

## Reading: Victory for voices over keystrokes

Point out this reading article to your students as "food for thought" when it comes to discussing the newest trends in customer service.

|   |   | True | False |
|---|---|---|---|
| 1 | *Netflix* customers can call the call center to order films which they then download. |  | ✓ |
| 2 | *Blockbuster* is *Netflix's* most important competitor. | ✓ |  |
| 3 | *Netflix* processes most of its customer enquiries by phone. |  | ✓ |
| 4 | More and more companies are outsourcing their services to external suppliers as well as moving services abroad. | ✓ |  |
| 5 | Most companies in the service sector provide customer service through call centers. |  | ✓ |
| 6 | *Blockbuster* does not operate a call center. |  | ✓ |
| 7 | *Netflix* decided against locating in Phoenix, Salt Lake City and Las Vegas because the cost of maintaining call centers there is high. |  | ✓ |
| 8 | Ms Funk is one of the newest employees at *Netflix*. |  | ✓ |

# 4 Selling to the consumer

### Self Study

**Vocabulary**
- Adjectives describing products, location and prices
- Types of retailers and their products
- Frequently confused words: *account for* and *amount to*

**Grammar**
- Adjectives: by comparison
- Adverbs: comparatively speaking
- What's where in the supermarket: prepositions of location

**Skills**
- Then and now: comparing pie charts
- Bar charts: using approximations
- Making a presentation flow

**Reading**
- Supermarket strategies: true or false?
- Guess the meaning

## At a glance

The fast-moving and exciting world of retailing is reflected by the range of topics covered in this unit which opens by considering different models such as **big-box**, **department store** and **mom-and-pop** retailing before critically examining the success story of discount models in food retailing.

The unit also considers some of the technological developments currently taking place in the sector and examines the intercultural aspects of exporting retail business models. Students are asked to analyze consumer behavior and have to put themselves in the shoes of an enterprise looking for the right retailer in the U.S. market. The unit concludes by focussing on the classic consideration for retailers, namely **location**. Along the way, the unit also takes in the contemporary issue of **bricks and mortar** vs. **online retailing** and contrasts the relative performance of the supermarket and apparel retail sectors.

Due to the importance of data in any discussion about retailing, the unit's *Business Skills* section focuses on the depiction of data about retail markets in graphs and charts. Students are offered ample opportunity to practice language for discussing and describing bar and pie charts.

For comprehensive coverage of developments in the retail sector, refer to the U.K.-based website:
www.retail-week.com

For a humorous take on retail, see this cartoon series created by a former retail manager:
www.normfeuticartoons.com/retail

## Warm-up

Before playing the listening, ensure that your students understand the word wholesaler. If necessary, point out a wholesaler sells to retailers, not directly to the public.

Now play the listening and collect answers around the class.

1 C mail order company    4 B department store
2 D mom-and-pop store    5 A big-box retailer
3 E specialty chain outlet

Ask the students to work with their neighbor to complete the second part of the exercise. Again check answers in open class.

1 C, 2 A, 3 D, 4 E, 5 B

Be sure to point out to students that *bricks and mortar* is used to describe retailers who still use shops in the traditional sense as opposed to selling by means of the internet.

Open up the final question to the whole class, writing suggestions in columns on the board under the five different headings.

1 Mail order companies: *Quelle, Otto, Neckermann*
2 Mom-and-pop stores: *Tante Emma-Läden*
3 Specialty chain outlet: *Douglas, H&M*
4 Department store: *Galeria Kaufhof*
5 Big-box retailer: *Real*

# 4 Selling to the consumer

## Reading: Discount food chains

**1** Divide your students into pairs for this exercise. They should discuss the questions taking note of what their partners say for reporting back to the class. Give them between five to ten minutes for this, then bring the class back together. Ask several students to report what their partner said about their shopping habits. Be sure to ask for examples which illustrate their choices in question 3. Ask students to elaborate on what factors comprise the *shopping experience* and note their ideas on the board.

**2** Ensure that students understand that they are to read the article only with a view to answering the three questions. This is a scan reading exercise during which they should not get bogged down in vocabulary they don't understand. Collect answers around the class.

> 1 The proliferation of discount food retailers outside of their country of origin and the fact that such discounters are rapidly winning market share at the expense of more traditional, high-end food retailers is evidence of the global price war as is the fact that the latter are cutting prices in an attempt to fight back.
> 2 The current winners of the price war are the discount food retailers. They are very successful in the global price war since cost savings are achieved by cheap shop layout, own-label products and a limited range of products. They quickly adapt to the tastes of the more affluent consumer by offering branded goods or fresh produce and delicatessen items.
> 3 The secret of their success is that they manage to leverage impressive economies of scale by stocking basic ranges of products which are bought in bulk. Additionally, they specialize in own-brand products which are more profitable for them to sell than branded foodstuffs.

**3** Your students should now read the article again and answer the true/false questions. Before they do so, point out that they should gather information from the article with which to justify their answers. Collect answers in open class.

> 1 **false**, 2 **false**, 3 **true**, 4 **false**, 5 **true**,
> 6 **true**, 7 **false**, 8 **false**, 9 **false**, 10 **false**

**4** Divide your students into new pairs for the following two exercises. They should collaborate in reading the article in order to find the target expressions.

> **Positive:** *sales are booming, taking market share, increased their market share, expand rapidly*
>
> **Negative:** *as economic prospects worsen, whereas the share fell at, is under pressure, has experienced one big setback, pulled out of*

**5**
1  the world's fourth-biggest retailer
2  a tenth of the market
3  a fraction
4  some 30 % of the market
5  have annual sales estimated at € 43 billion and €35 billion respectively

**6** Prepare your students for this task by asking if anyone knows anything about the story of *Wal-Mart* in Germany. Make a list of all the true facts on the board. Then encourage students to research the story of *Wal-Mart* in Germany on the internet. For instance, they could search for 'Wal-Mart failure in Germany'.

In the next lesson, they should be prepared to recount the story in summary form and discuss their conclusions.

> *Wal-Mart* made mistakes which might be considered intercultural in nature and which resulted in a retreat from Germany in 2006. However, there were other, more business-related reasons.
> First of all, *Wal-Mart* had entered the market through acquiring the German retail chains *Wertkauf* and *Spar*, a strategy which was flawed from the beginning, as these chains had included many unprofitable locations. Furthermore, *Wal-Mart* had failed to understand German labor legislation and the power of German unions. Thirdly, *Wal-Mart* had underestimated the ability of its major German competitors – *Aldi*, *Lidl*, *Rewe* and *Edeka* – to defend their position by matching all of *Wal-Mart's* price cuts and at the same time providing superior customer service.

34

## Listening: **The lowest prices around**

**1** Tell your students that their first task is simply to listen for the five prices mentioned. Give them a few moments to read over the information they are required to listen for before playing CD track 14.

1. $13.99
2. $10.29
3. $2.29
4. $0.99
5. $87.00

**2** Draw your students' attention to the two questions and ensure that they focus on listening for information which answers these questions before playing the second section of the interview with Brad Allan again. After the listening, ask students to spend a few minutes comparing their answers with those of their neighbor before bringing the class back together to check their answers.

1. The retailer offers branded goods at lower prices than its competitor. This is in contrast to German retailers' own-brand strategy.

2. He mentions cutting the costs of warehousing and logistics, lowering profit margins and establishing long-term relationships with suppliers which result in lower wholesale prices.

3. Discuss this question with the whole class. Students can often be fairly skeptical about the means by which the price of retail goods are kept down. Expect them to come up with issues such as wage and job cuts, pressure on unions, hiring unskilled workers and relying on child labor in developing countries as reasons for low prices. However, should they require some prompting, ask them to think about what it may be like to work on the shop floor for *Best Bargain*. And what about those suppliers mentioned in the interview which have gone out of business as a result of pressure on prices? What might working life be like for the employees of suppliers who succeed in maintaining their relationship with *Best Bargain*? Finally, might there be implications for the quality of goods produced and sold according to such a low price model?

## Discussion: **The future of retailing**

Divide your students into small groups. Ask them to read the information about the three pieces of technology before discussing the questions in their groups. Draw attention to the language box on the right of the page and encourage your students to use the phrases as often as possible during their discussion. Each group should choose a note-taker to take notes on the discussion.

When the discussion is over, get a member of each group to report back. Open up the final question to the whole class, prompting as many students as possible to contribute their ideas.

The **barcode** has changed retailing in that it has shortened check out times dramatically resulting in a speedier experience for customers. It has also automated stock-taking and re-ordering processes and, in so doing, slashed the number of man-hours required. This has resulted in lower staffing levels. In many modern retailers, stock-taking and re-ordering take place at the point of sale. The can of baked beans you just bought has been automatically taken off the shop's inventory and information about the sale will also automatically contribute to the next call up of baked beans from the warehouse or supplier.

Both the **Shopping Buddy** and the **Interactive Shelf-Talker** result in lower staff levels. The more information at the customers' fingertips, the less need for shop floor staff. This could also result in increased sales because customers have information with which to inform their purchasing decisions and no longer need to hunt for members of staff to put their questions to. Retailers typically lose large numbers of sales during the time that it takes to drum up a shop assistant to answer a question and customers get cold feet about making their purchase.

The **Self-Check-Out Machine** clearly results in the need for less check out staff and may increase sales to customers who feel that they can complete the check out process more swiftly on their own.

All of these technologies probably address the needs of young, tech-savvy consumers who have grown accustomed to the endless wealth of information provided by the internet. Disadvantages of these technologies to the retailer might include the relatively high cost of purchase, installation and maintenance as well as loss of sales to customers who may feel over-powered by information over-load and the lack of shop assistants who might otherwise have offered the "personal touch".

# 4 Selling to the consumer

**6** Retailing race board game

Use the board game to give your students additional practice in the phrases used for speculating at the bottom of page 37 in the Course Book.

Split the students into groups of four or five giving each student a set of 10 cut up cards and each group a game board. Each group will also need a coin and each player a token to use as a playing piece.

The first player tosses the coin (heads = move one square; tails = move two squares. 'Tails' is the side of the coin which shows its value.) S/he then has to speculate about the development described in the square using one of the cards from their set. After using this card, it is laid to the side and cannot be used again. Then it's the next player's turn. Should more than one player land on the same square the second and successive players to do so have to come up with a fresh speculation about the statement in the square using one of their phrase cards. You may want to set a time limit of about 20 seconds for each player to come up with their speculation. More able students could be given slightly less time for this. The first player to reach the *Finish* square is the winner. However, allow the other players to continue until everyone has completed the board.

Listen in while the groups are playing and take note of some particularly insightful speculations. At the end of the game repeat them to the class inviting students to comment upon them and allow a few minutes for discussion.

## Business Skills

## Charts: **Understanding bar and pie charts**

**1** Before putting your students into pairs to consider the charts, you will need to make it clear that *Costco* is a supermarket and *Walgreens* a drug store, while *Abercrombie & Fitch* and *American Eagle* are clothing retailers. Give the pairs between five and ten minutes to consider the charts and their answers to the questions before collecting answers in open class.

1 Roughly one quarter of this amount was generated by *Wal-Mart* alone. The other quarter is shared among the top nine U.S. retailers, whereas the remaining half is shared among the rest of the 90 retailers.
2 In general, there is larger revenue growth in the apparel segment than in the supermarket segment. Only in the organic food segment are higher rates recorded.
3 Chart 3 shows the 40 hottest retailers in the U.S. by revenue growth between 2004/07. None of the supermarkets are in the top quartile. Chart 3 shows that companies that have the highest revenues may not be experiencing the highest growth rates. For example, *Wal-Mart* was the number one retailer by revenue in 2007 (chart 1) but ranked 39th in terms of revenue growth in the same year (chart 3).

**2** Before playing the listening, make it clear to your students that they are only to listen for the information missing in the sentences. They should not concern themselves with other elements of the listening which they don't immediately understand. Collect answers in open class. Write the correct words and phrases on the board as the students call them out. Having done this, ask the students to close their Course Books and quiz them. This should help them consolidate the language in the exercise. Put your students into three or four teams, then go through each of the words or phrases on the board. The students' task is to present the statistical facts described in the listening using the words or phrases. Award a point to the first group which can relate the statistical fact on each occasion correctly. The wording used does not have to be identical to the sentences from the lecture. However the use of the phrase has to be correct.

1 *Wal-Mart* tops the list by far with $379 billion, which is well over a fourth of all revenue combined.
2 Although the pie chart shows only the ten most successful retailers in the U.S., one thing is rather striking.
3 *Costco's* and *Target's* revenue amount to roughly $64 million each.
4 *Supervalue*, which ranks tenth, has revenue of $44 million, which is less than 12% of *Wal-Mart's* revenue.
5 Its growth rate is more than twice that of *Wal-Mart*.
6 *American Apparel* showed the fifth highest growth rate.
7 None of the supermarkets are in the top quartile.
8 Only the whole food seller *Whole Foods Market* outperforms them – with 70.6%.

## Selling to the consumer — 4

## Charts: **Describing bar and pie charts**

Divide your students into pairs. *Student As* should now open their books at page 124 and *Student Bs* to page 134. The students should take a few minutes to study the charts as well as the *Useful expressions* list on page 166.

While students are describing the graphs in their pairs, circulate and listen in for mistakes and check that the templates are being completed correctly.

## Diversity: **Consumer behavior across cultures**

Before dividing your students into small groups to work on this exercise, ask them to scan read the factors that they are to take into account. Also ask them to speculate about how the American market may differ from theirs in these respects. Comment on what you take to be the accuracy of their perceptions, writing up keywords on the board to assist them in their discussion.

The groups should now consider how these factors as applied to the North American market would affect the decisions of a food retailer before moving on to consider the French case.

They should take notes on the results of their discussion to help them report back to the class later.

Listen in on the discussions and attempt to identify two groups which reach different conclusions as to the implications of at least some of the factors. When the group discussion phase is over, ask the groups to present their results inviting students from other groups to comment. A fruitful discussion should arise.

## Role-play: **Choosing the right distribution channel**

Tell your students which of them will play *A*, *B*, *C* and *D* and split them into four groups each containing only students playing the same roles. Make it clear to the students that this is a preparation phase which will help them get ready for the role-play. The students should now read over the situation box, study their roles and look over the notes and charts about the six retailers. Having done this, they should spend some five minutes discussing the role they are to play and, in the light of this, which of the retailers they would recommend as well as their reasons for their choice.

At this stage, remind your students of the language for describing and discussing charts which they encountered on page 39 and that for speculating about future developments on page 37. Encourage them to use several of these phrases in the course of the role-play.

Now split the students into their role-playing groups. Given the extensive nature of the material that they are to discuss, allow the students up to 25 minutes for the role-play. Conclude the exercise by bringing the class back together and inviting students to report on the decisions they've agreed upon. Allow the groups to briefly discuss their decisions.

Students will come to their own conclusions but might want to consider the following:
*Best Bargain* has the highest market share but growth is stagnating, possibly because the chain does not provide a pleasant shopping experience. *Best Bargain* seems to pay decent wages (by U.S. standards) but the amount of merchandise sold per employee suggests that the stores are understaffed.
*BigMart* appears to be in a crisis. It has had negative sales growth and is trying to turn itself around.
Although *Matt's Market* and *Green Goddess Foods* have a relatively small market share, they have impressive growth rates and the shopping experience they provide seems to be valued by their customers. *Matt's Market* pays its employees well. All of this suggests that the chain has an up-market clientele and a good image. The shopping experience at *Green Goddess Foods* receives an even higher rating and the chain has the highest growth rate of all the chains, although of the six chains mentioned it has the smallest market share. The question for *SuperStrudel* is whether their goal is to achieve a high volume with a mass merchandiser or position themselves up-market. Ethical considerations are probably also important to *SuperStrudel* (cf. their own business model) and some of the retailers don't pay their employees well.

# 4 Selling to the consumer

## Company Case: **The right part of town**

Divide your students into new groups for this exercise, then get them thinking about different types of retail location by drawing a circle on the board and writing *city center* in it. Ask the class what other parts of town shops can be located in and assist with specific words and phrases, for instance, *edge-of-town retail parks and shopping malls*. Write the suggestions on the board.

Now ask the students to scan read the text and establish the variety of retail environments which *Winstead* has. Be sure that they understand what an outlet mall is. When they have finished reading, ask two or three students to summarize this information.

Now let the students discuss the case. Make it clear that each group should choose one member to take notes so that they can report back to the class. Allow up to 15 minutes for the group discussions before bringing the class back together. Ask a member of each group to present the recommendations arising from the discussion.

# Over to you

## Writing: Summarizing information

Prepare your students for this task by brainstorming with the class what form such a memo would take. It would open with a clear, short, "structuring" paragraph which would outline what it considers and the recommendations it makes. After presentation of the arguments in summary form, the memo would conclude by again repeating its recommendations. Its language would probably be quite sparse and the information could be presented in a series of bullet points.

## Web research: Online retailing

Given the depth the students are required to go into in their analysis of the retailer's web presence, you may choose to assign each student the task of considering only one retailer. Do this by getting the class to brainstorm a list of bricks and mortal retailers which also sell online and assign each student one retailer. You might also extend the exercise by asking students to consider the probable reasons for differences between a retailer's bricks and mortar and online offers. The possible answers here will depend on the individual retailers and their product ranges.

## Reading: Big Retailers still struggle in India

1 She is typical of many other Indians in that she views large, modern retail outlets as being worth visiting, but only purely out of interest rather than the desire to buy there. She prefers to make her purchases in small, privately-owned shops which offer personalized service.
2 Large, foreign retailers are restricted in that they have to partner up with Indian companies in order to sell in the wholesale sector rather than sell directly to consumers.
3 Loyalty to mom-and-pop stores can be explained by the personal service, the low prices and the fact that purchases on tab are possible.
4 Indian chains have not been much more successful than their Western equivalents because they also lack the personal touch, which is so important to Indians.
5 Answers will vary.

# 5 Globalization and international trade

## At a glance

Globalization has resulted in some of the most profound economic paradigm shifts of recent decades: this unit will equip your students to voice their opinions about its impact whether they are optimistic or skeptical as to its benefits.

The unit begins by prompting students to define globalization and discuss the pros and cons of the phenomenon. The reading which follows furnishes students with a vocabulary set – including terms such as **tariffs**, **quotas**, **subsidies** and **balance of payments** – which they can use to discuss the controlling mechanisms of international trade. Also touched upon in the reading are the social consequences of globalization both in developed and developing countries which provides students with key pieces of lexis such as **ripple effect**, **watershed** and **social safety net**. Students are then invited to consider the impact of globalization on labor markets and discuss the offshoring of jobs from developed to developing economies.

The unit then looks at how goods are shipped across the globe in an examination of the revolution brought about in shipping by containerization. In this section of the unit, students' vocabulary resources are enriched further by the inclusion of terms such as **customs**, **duty**, **freight**, **haulage**, **storage** and **vessel**.

In the *Business Skills* section the focus is initially on telephoning: the context for this a problem with a **bill of lading**. Of course, deals between companies from different parts of the globe, irrespective of how big or small they may be, rely upon establishing personal rapport between individuals. Small talk, therefore, is the next area of focus for students: this is also the main topic covered in the video episode which accompanies the unit.

Students get the chance to put into practice what they have learned about small talk in the role-play which concentrates on a tricky social situation that will force your students to think – and talk – on their feet. The *Company Case* rounds the unit off with an examination of one aspect of what can go wrong for Western companies in manufacturing partnerships with companies from developing countries and encourages students to work on strategic solutions.

For further general background information on globalization see:
http://www.globalpolicy.org/globalization.html

For regularly updated articles about trends in and debates about globalization see:
http://yaleglobal.yale.edu/

For discussion about how globalization can be harnessed to the end of alleviating poverty see:
http://www.globalenvision.org/?gclid=CLLjkaafw5sCFcITzAod7DQndw

## Self Study

**Vocabulary**
- Finding words in the same family
- Using the language of trade and transport
- Using the right verbs: from warehouse to customer

**Grammar**
- Using prepositions of time
- Using the right form: econo-
- Tense practice: Sourcing then and now

**Skills**
- Complaining in a business situation
- Apologizing for a mistake or an inconvenience
- Small talk: who says what?

**Reading**
- Reading comprehension: doing business in a flat world
- Text/sentence reconstruction: Putting it back together

**Video**
- Not at a loss for words: what to talk about
- What did they actually say?
- Meeting new people
- The art of socializing

## Warm-up

Write the sentence parts onto cards giving sets of these to small groups of students. Should you wish to up the level of challenge for your class – or for some more able students in particular – break the sentence down further on the cards.

Globalization is the worldwide process in which goods, services and capital move across national borders to other markets resulting in an interconnected international market.

# 5 Globalization and international trade

The definition makes no reference to migration and culture. Moreover, globalization has some negative connotations, particularly for younger people, who might see it as being exploitative of developing countries and environmentally damaging, increasing as it has global industrial output. Some students may feel that these aspects of globalization are missing from the definition.

Should the discussion arising from the final part of the warm-up become lengthy and heated and you would like your students to do some further thinking, invite individual students to carry out research about their views on the internet, the results of which could be presented and briefly discussed at the next class.

## Reading: Trouble with Trade

**1** Pair off your students. Before they complete the mind map, allow the pairs a moment to identify potentially difficult vocabulary which they should attempt to explain to one another before turning to you. Be prepared to explain *tariffs*, *quotas*, *subsidies*, *sweatshops* and *balance of payments deficit*.

Introduce an element of competition and classroom movement into the completion of the mind map by copying it from the Course Book onto the board. Tell the pairs that they are to race each other to complete it. They should do this first in their books, then run to the board to complete it there. Those students at the board first will have to fight for space though, as other students join them in their efforts to complete the mind map quickly. Make sure there are lots of marker pens to hand to allow each student the chance to contribute. When they have finished, confirm that the students have completed the mind map correctly.

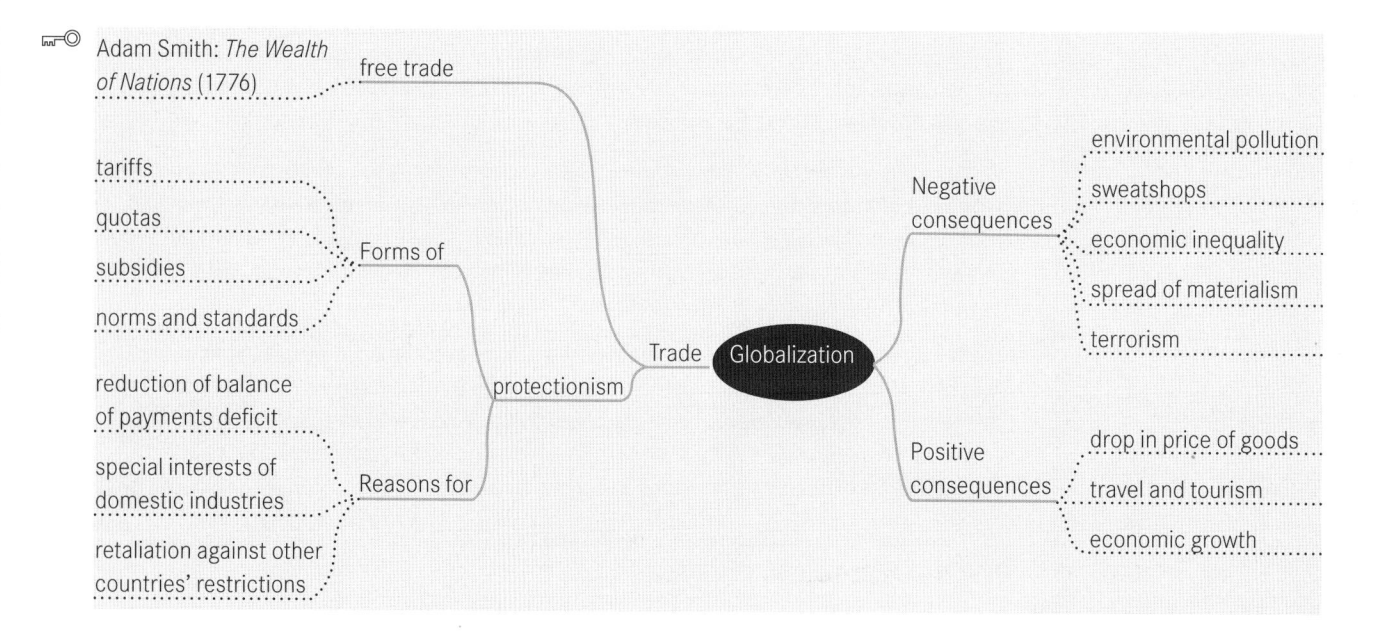

Adam Smith: *The Wealth of Nations* (1776)

- free trade
- tariffs
- quotas
- subsidies
- norms and standards

**Forms of** — Trade — **Globalization**

- reduction of balance of payments deficit
- special interests of domestic industries
- retaliation against other countries' restrictions

**Reasons for** protectionism

**Negative consequences**
- environmental pollution
- sweatshops
- economic inequality
- spread of materialism
- terrorism

**Positive consequences**
- drop in price of goods
- travel and tourism
- economic growth

**2** 1 d, 2 c, 3 e, 4 b, 5 a

**3** Give the pairs two minutes to brainstorm the aspects of international trade which people might be troubled by. While they are doing this, draw a two-column table with the headings aspect and negative consequences on the board. Have a couple of examples up your sleeve to get things going should the students be short of ideas: for instance, how the purchasing power of Western companies can cause primary producers from the developing world to accept low prices for their produce. Bring the class back together and write your students' suggestions on the board.

**4**

**Effects of global trade on the U.S. economy**

**benefits**
- The car industry has been able to increase productivity and wages.
- Highly skilled workers have higher wages and better job opportunities.
- *Wal-Mart* is able to offer lower prices to its customers.

**drawbacks**
- Some high tech workers have lost jobs to companies in India.
- Less skilled workers have lost their jobs to workers overseas.
- They then press into industries where similar qualifications are needed, bringing wages down there.

# Globalization and international trade 5

**5** As the students have now read the article in detail individually, pair them up to work on questions 5 and 7, encouraging them to collaborate in finding evidence in the article and writing the answers. To assist students in identifying the shifts in the article between positive and negative aspects of trade, ask them to highlight these with different colored highlighters. You might consider setting some pairs the task of answering question 5 while others work on the answer to question 7. Should you do this, spend a little more time on an open class discussion of the answers giving students a chance to exchange information about how they answered the questions.

Finally, ask your students to investigate the language of Krugman's argument more thoroughly by setting them the task of identifying which "connecting" expressions he uses as he shifts from positive to negative aspects of trade and on to his conclusion, i. e. he uses *but* and *however* to indicate the shift from positive to negative and the rhetorical question *So, am I arguing for protectionism?* to indicate the beginning of his conclusion.

For the world economy as a whole Krugman does think globalization is a good thing. He points out, however, that there are always those who do not benefit from it and that the social safety net should be strengthened in order to take care of these people.
He qualifies his statements, e. g. *a modest win*, *on balance*, *it is at least arguable*.
He vacillates between the two points of view, using words and expressions such as *but / still / by contrast / the trouble is ...*
Indeed, the article's title *Trouble with Trade* is a play on words which alludes both to the problems associated with trade and the social discord which arises from it.

**6** The trouble with trade is that while the world economy as a whole profits, there are large groups of people, e.g. less qualified workers in the industrialized countries, who do not.

**7** Whereas the U.S. (and other industrialized countries) used to import largely raw materials from developing countries and manufactured goods from other industrialized countries, most manufactured goods are now imported from poorer nations.
Krugman used to feel that everyone benefited from trade. Now he is prepared to recognize that there are large groups of losers as well as winners.

**8** It may be the case that many of the points – and particularly the drawbacks – have already been raised in the warm-up exercise on page 41. Based on what you remember from this discussion of your students' views about globalization, split them into groups of those who take a critical view and those who take a more positive view. Set the critics the task of thinking of as many benefits as possible and give the second group the job of coming up with as many drawbacks as they can. When they are finished, consolidate their lists on the board assisting with formulation as you do so. Round up with a whole-class discussion.

Developing economies:
**Benefits:** job creation, increased prosperity, economic growth
**Drawbacks:** possible exploitation of workers, environmental degradation, loss of traditions and culture

Students will find other points as well – which is fine.

## Discussion: **Thinking about globalization**

**1** Split your students into groups. They may need a little prompting to get started on 1. Offer them the example of call centers in India which most will probably be aware of. You could do this as follows. Tell your students you're going to describe a common situation in the globalized world. Say *It's midday in New York. My computer stops working. I find the hotline number and dial it on the phone ... It's the middle of the night in Bangalore, India. The telephone rings ...* Ask your students *What happens next?*

The groups should now brainstorm a list of jobs which can be subject to outsourcing and a list of those which are not generally subject to it for the second question. Consolidate students' ideas on the board.

**2** highly specialized workers such as lawyers and doctors, workers with skills that will only be used locally (cooks, plumbers, masseurs, cleaners)

**3** Should some groups finish ahead of others in answering this question, set them the additional task of ranking the skills and abilities that they listed in order of importance. Alternatively, you might consider doing this as a whole-class activity for consolidation at the end. Get students to call out the points they came up with and write them on the board.

41

# 5 Globalization and international trade

🔑 According to Thomas Friedman in *The World is Flat*: the ability to learn, the ability to navigate and gather information from the web, passion and curiosity, the ability to think across disciplines, the ability to synthesize information from disparate disciplines, social skills such as the ability to collaborate with others.

Over and above this, young people would need to be able to communicate effectively in other languages and have a degree of cultural understanding of the people from other cultures who they come into contact with through their work.

## Listening: **The container revolution**

**1** 
🔑
1  The warehouse has hired an additional security guard because of the problem of <u>pilfering</u>.
2  Rail transport is often considerably faster than road <u>haulage</u>.
3  For some travelers, the <u>destination</u> is less important than the journey.
4  The aircraft is designed to carry <u>freight</u> as well as passengers.
5  The building is small and doesn't provide much space for <u>storage</u>.
6  The <u>customs</u> officers are on strike and refusing to check cargo flights.
7  There is no <u>duty</u> on goods coming from other countries within the E.U.
8  All items sent with express delivery will receive priority <u>handling</u>.
9  The <u>vessel</u> has a capacity of 1000 passengers and 306 cars.

**2** Warm up for this exercise by drawing your students' attention to the title of the listening and tell them that they are going to hear a business report on the radio which is about the "container revolution". Ask the class to speculate about what might be included in the radio report, prompting them if necessary. Write their responses on the board. Now ask them to listen in order to hear if their speculations proved correct. Get one or two students to summarize the report briefly in general terms.

Allow students a minute or so to read through the statements. When they have completed the exercise, check their answers in open class.

🔑 1 **false**, 2 **false**, 3 **false**, 4 **false**, 5 **false**, 6 **true**

**3** Before the students complete this exercise, check quickly that they remember what *used to* means by writing a sentence featuring the construction on the board: *I used to smoke but I gave up in 2001 and haven't had a single cigarette since.*

Ask the students to write a sentence about themselves using *used to,* then get them to call out their sentences. Now tell them to listen to track 17 again and to take notes of the information they need. Tell them they will have time afterwards to write up their notes into full sentences. Check answers in open class.

🔑
- Loading the goods used to take a long time, but today it can be done very quickly.
- Ports used to need a lot of workers, while today very few are required.
- Ports used to have large warehouses, but today that is seldom necessary.
- Lots of goods used to be damaged or stolen while stored in warehouses, but today that risk is much lower, as goods usually remain in the containers.

**4** Pair off your students for 4 and 5 and collect answers to both questions in open class, writing the students' suggestions on the board. As they do not receive the information directly from the listening which they need to complete 4, but need to "listen between the lines" a little, you may need to prompt your students here. Ask an opening question to get them going, *Are containers robust or fragile? Are they easy to transport?*

🔑
- heavy duty construction (protects goods)
- available in different sizes
- stackable
- standardized

**5**
🔑
- for storage purposes
- offices
- accommodation (housing, tourism)
- bridges
- garages

42

# Globalization and international trade 5

## Business Skills

### Telephoning: Business to business (B2B)

**1** Before playing the listening, ensure that your students have read and understand the information they are looking for. Call on individual students to summarize this in their own words. Repeat the listening should a significant number of students not be in a position to answer the questions after the first run through.

1 16 March
2 21 February
3 9 March
4 18 days
5 $880
6 special handling for sensitive equipment

**2** Split your students into pairs for this exercise and ask them to explain what they think a *bill of lading* is. Familiarize your students with the basic vocabulary of the *Bill of Lading* by writing *shipper*, *consignee* and *carrier* on the board and asking them to look at the document and decide which party is which. If you feel that you have time, ask your students to explore the bill of lading further for the other information that it contains. Much of this is already referred to in exercise 1. However, the document contains other important information, for example, how many copies of the document have been produced, its number and how the shipment will be paid for.

Do not play the listening again before doing the exercise if you have already played it twice but allow students to tackle it on the basis of what they remember. As you monitor their progress in identifying the mistakes in the document, you may opt to play the track again should the students be struggling with the exercise.

**Mistakes on the Bill of Lading:**

| | |
|---|---|
| the name of the vessel | the Endeavour, not the Victory |
| the port of loading | Felixstowe, not Southampton |
| the port of discharge | Houston, not Galveston |
| the address of the consignee | The company is in Houston, not Dallas |
| the description of the commodity | engineering equipment, not fluorescent lights |
| the consignee | Thetis Shipping, not Mapet Engineering |
| the shipper | Mapet Engineering, not TDM Engineering |

**3** Start by asking the students to read the checklist on their own to identify which points on it might be important for Adam Grimm as he makes his phone call. Get one or two students to comment on this.

To ensure that your students get as much as possible from the role-play, prepare them as follows. Split them into two groups: those who will be Adam Grimm (Group A) and those who will play the Thetis employee (Group B). Set Group B the task of thinking how they will answer the telephone: they should give their name, the company name and offer to be of assistance. While they are working on this formulation, move to Group A and ask the students to think of how they will introduce themselves on the phone: they should state their name, company and the reason for their call. Additionally, draw their attention to the language box. Tell them that they are to think about how to formulate their various complaints about the mistakes on the bill of lading using the softening phrases given.

Now return to Group B. Ask a couple of students to say their introductory sentence, then introduce the following phrases for apologizing to the students:

- *I'm sorry to hear that we have made some mistakes.*
- *Please accept my apologies for this.*
- *I'll change the bill of lading immediately.*
- *Once again, I'm sorry to hear that ...*
- *Sorry for any inconvenience this has caused.*

Ask the students to write these on strips of paper and to aim to use at least three of these during the role-play. Having used one of the phrases, students should turn the strip of paper over.

Return to Group A again asking students to state the points they will make on the phone using the phrases from the language box. Having confirmed that they can use the phrases appropriately, split the class into pairs. Tell the pairs to place two chairs back to back so that they can sit close to each other during the role-play but cannot make eye contact.

Monitor the students as they carry out the role-play, taking note of any mistakes that you might want to pick up on at the end. If you have the time, ask the pair which you felt performed the role-play most successfully to repeat it for the other students. Round off by bringing the class back together, congratulating the students on their efforts and focusing on two or three mistakes which you want to highlight. Elicit corrections from the students.

### Solving a problem by phone

Hand out a copy of the dialog cut into strips to each pair. Explain that this is a telephone conversation similar to the one they have just role-played. Their task is to reassemble it. You might choose to turn this into a race: the first pair to reassemble the conversation successfully

# 5 Globalization and international trade

wins. After you have confirmed the order of the conversation by asking the winning pair to read it out, give the students one minute to underline what they think might be standard telephone expressions, *Sara Jones speaking. How can I help you?*, phrases for apologizing *Please accept my apologies for* ... and phrases for softening criticism *I'm afraid there are one or two mistakes on it* ... Round off by getting the students to call these out. Encourage them to record them in their notebooks.

## Small talk: **Saying the right thing**

**1** Split your students into pairs setting them the task of discussing the three questions. Ask them to make a list of appropriate small talk topics and the reasons why business people make small talk. Put a time limit of five minutes on the discussion.

Bring the class back together and ask the students to call out small-talk topics they think are appropriate – one student should write these up on the board.

Be careful not to dismiss points on the list out of hand. You should make the point to students that attitudes to small talk differ between cultures and that it is worth researching a little into the attitudes of people from specific cultures before doing business with them. Discuss with your students what they might want to talk about. Emphasize that there are no hard and fast rules when it comes to making small talk, only tendencies.

**2** The students return to their pairs. Ask them to spend a few minutes coming up with appropriate responses to the statements and questions. Then bring the class back together. Read out the first statement, *My name is Colin Finn* and prompt the students to call out their responses. Write these on the board gently correcting any mistakes and offering responses which might be idiomatically more commonplace than some of the students' suggestions. Continue this with all the statements and questions until you have written all the students' responses up. Allow the class some time to note down all the responses.

**3** Before the students listen, make the point that they don't need to copy the responses word for word. Advise them to check in the audioscript for exact wording after class.

**4** Get your students to call out what Colin says and then ask them if they know any other ways of saying the same thing.

1 He says that he likes the restaurant very much using the word <u>fantastic</u>.
2 He states his lack of interest in temples by saying that he's <u>not interested in history</u>.
3 He says that the food tastes very good, ... <u>this is very tasty</u>.

Synonyms:
1 great; wonderful; lovely
2 I don't care too much for history
3 delicious; lovely

**5** Play the listening and ask the students to call out what they heard.

● Mr Finn, it's <u>been a pleasure</u> having <u>you</u> at *Infosystems*. I do hope we've <u>been able</u> to <u>provide you</u> with all the information you need.
■ Yes, <u>you certainly have</u>, Mr Kumarswami. It's <u>been a very</u> fruitful <u>visit</u>. And thank you so much <u>for your hospitality</u>.
● It <u>was our pleasure</u>. Give my <u>best regards</u> to your wife.

**Video: An internship abroad: Socializing and small talk**
You may choose to use the video clip at this stage.

Before playing the clip, ask your students to bear these questions in mind:

- *What advice does Harold give Rebecca about suitable topics for small talk with the visitor?*
- *How successful is she in establishing rapport with the visitor through small talk?*
- *Does she handle the situation well?*

Invite your students to discuss the questions. Ask if there is anything which Rebecca might learn about making small talk from her experience of greeting the visitor.

# Globalization and international trade 5

## Diversity
### Role-play: Small talk or deep talk?

Before splitting your students into pairs, tell each student which role they will play. Ask the students to read their role-play file and allow them sufficient time for this. While they are reading, circulate and discreetly answer questions about vocabulary which they may have. Make sure to do this quietly with individual students: the success of the role-play depends upon secrecy about the nature of the opposing roles.

Now split the students briefly into two groups at far ends of the classroom. Check that they understand their roles properly, ensure that *Student A*s know they are to resist prolonged attempts at small talk and should repeatedly return to the subject of climate control. *Student B*s should be clear that they are to make repeated attempts at small talk: they should have several topics in mind in order to keep the conversation moving in this direction.

The students then carry out the role-play. Monitor what the students are saying and note down good examples of how they formulate their various attempts either to talk shop or make small talk. Allow up to 15 minutes for the role-play but be prepared to end the exercise after this time even if the students are still speaking.

Round off with a discussion about what might be concluded from the role-play about cultural differences between the U.S. and the students' own country in open class. Be wary about allowing the students to draw conclusions which are too rigid. Students will not only have to develop their understanding of other cultures but also their ability to empathize with people from these cultures as individuals.

## Company Case: Children at risk

Split your students into small groups. Prepare them for the case study by drawing their attention to the headline, *Children at risk*, and reading out the opening passage. Ask the groups to discuss for three minutes what they think the article might be about and which points it might include. When they have finished, get them to call out their suggestions and write these on the board.

The students should now read the article in their groups. When they are finished invite questions about vocabulary and be prepared to explain *recall*, *outsource*, *concern*, *swallow* and *intestinal perforation*.

Now ask the students to work in their groups and think of reasons for the flaws in the toys. After five minutes get them to call out their suggestions.

### Trade talk board game

Review key lexis featured in the unit by getting your students to play the board game. Split the class into pairs giving each a copy of the game. Check that each pair has three coins to play the game with. Two of these are playing pieces. The other coin is to be used in place of a die. The coin should be tossed (heads = one move; tails = two moves. 'Tails' is the side of the coin that shows its value.)
If a player lands on a:
- **Finish the sentence** square, they have to fill the gap/s with an appropriate expression from the unit.
- **Soften this** square, they have to reiterate the statement in less direct terms using an expression from page 48 or the *Useful expressions*.
- **Make small talk** square, they have to offer an appropriate small-talk response to the question or statement
- **Quick task** square, they have to complete the set task in the time specified.
- **Trade places** square, they have to trade places with their partner's playing piece.

If a player gets a question right, they can move forward a square before the other player takes their turn. Should they get a question wrong, they move back a square. Be on hand to adjudicate in the event of students not being able to reach agreement about whether a given answer is correct.

- Lax standards in the factories of Chinese suppliers
- Possibly pressure to meet deadlines (workers are paid on a piece-work basis, required to work at great speed)

Each of the groups should now choose and discuss one of the options open to the company. Try to ensure that each option is investigated by a group. The groups should elect a spokesperson to report their findings after the discussions which you should allow them ten minutes to complete. Be prepared to supplement their suggestions with some of your own.

# 5 Globalization and international trade

**Returning production to the U.S.**

| | |
|---|---|
| advantages | • would create jobs in the U.S. (good PR for company) |
| | • would increase *PlayWorld's* credibility for consumer |
| | • would give *PlayWorld* a competitive advantage in terms of reputation and business ethics |
| | • would greatly reduce probability that such flaws would occur again |
| disadvantages | • would be extremely cost-intensive; however, recalls and class action suits are also very expensive |

**Industry alliance**

| | |
|---|---|
| advantages | • cheaper than returning production to the U.S. |
| | • may prove more credible to consumer than internal monitoring |
| disadvantages | • would require time to organize |
| | • would require that *PlayWorld* cooperate with competitors |

**Pressure on suppliers**

| | |
|---|---|
| advantages | • would regard minimum investment |
| | • company could employ internal monitors |
| disadvantages | • not likely to calm consumers |
| | • likelihood that, after an initial improvement, suppliers will revert to old standards is great |

Bring the class back together for a discussion about which option or combination of options might be best for the company.

## Over to you

### Writing: Wealth through trade

**1** If you have already covered Unit 4, refer the students to pages 38–39 where they examined how to describe charts. Remind them that, in addition to using the expressions in the language box on page 52, they could also use the expressions covered in Unit 4 to describe the graph.

Additionally, remind your students that a graph description would not only consist of the detailed description of year upon year developments, but usually starts with a sentence summarizing in general terms the information that is going to be discussed. A graph description should end with a conclusion which again summarizes the information in different terms. Make it clear to students that the use of such devices will add to the power of their writing.

**2** Again stress the importance of students structuring their essay. Before they start writing, ensure that you draw the students' attention to the language box and restate the importance of the expressions for structuring the flow of an argument. Encourage your students to use as many expressions from the box as possible.

If you have time, invite your students to email both the description of the graph and their short essay to you so you can add comments and return them. It's worth remembering to compliment students on successful essay structure and the use of structuring language, i. e. *moreover*, *however* as well as to offer corrections of any mistakes they may have made.

### Web activity: Researching trade policies

**1** You could split students into four groups which should each research the current trade policies of one of the regions or countries mentioned. The students could present their findings briefly and informally at the next class.

Should you wish to structure your students' search so that it eliminates the hundreds of ultra-left and ultra-right anti-globalization websites on the internet, you could suggest they visit the following websites:

*ATTAC* is a global network of activists who, though claiming not to be against globalization as such, are outspoken in their criticisms of it in its current form. Its website is a good source for arguments against globalization.
www.attac.org

*War on Want* is a British-based charity which campaigns to end poverty in the developing world and the trade arrangements which it says lead to it.
http://www.waronwant.org/

*The Fairtrade Foundation* is an organization which opposes what it sees as the exploitation of primary producers in the developed world by multi-national companies.
http://www.fairtrade.org.uk/

# 6 Products and production

## Self Study

**Vocabulary**
- Talking about production
- Verbs used in production: be precise
- More production verbs

**Grammar**
- The passive: talking about production processes
- It's all relative!
- Past perfect or simple past: when did it happen?

**Skills**
- Describing a product: features and specifications
- What can your product do?
- Describing a production process

**Reading**
- The giant sucking sound: Reading for detail
- Extend your word power through reading

## At a glance

Despite the increasing trend among Western economies towards the development of service sector industries, manufacturing continues to play a major role. This unit reflects the continuing importance of manufacturing as well as current developments within the sector and will offer your students the nuts and bolts of the language they will need to discuss how contemporary business organizes production.

The unit presents vocabulary for describing **production methods** including **upstream** and **downstream processes**, **inventory**, **lead time** and **lean manufacturing**. It examines the extent to which older manufacturing paradigms are still viable and takes a close look at assembly line production. Students have the opportunity to practice describing production processes and discuss the conditions of work experienced by factory personnel. The relationship between production and **waste** is also examined in detail as are the changes in manufacturing brought about by globalization.

The *Business Skills* section focuses on the verbal and written presentation of product details: students get the chance to explore the kind of language used to describe product features both in presentations and writing, the emphasis here being on overcoming the challenge of producing interesting texts about potentially dry technical details.

The *Company Case* rounds the unit off with a discussion of almost global contemporary relevance to companies: whether to relocate production to low-wage countries in an attempt to drive down costs.

For manufacturing news and blog-based discussion about developments in the sector see:
http://www.industryweek.com/

For company case studies which will offer insight into the shifts taking place in manufacturing see:
http://www.themanufacturer.com/ Click on *Articles* and look for *company profiles*.

## Warm-up

Divide your students into groups and draw their attention to the definitions on the left of the page. After making sure that they understand their first task, give the groups five minutes to match the diagrams to the descriptions. Get students to call out the matches they made in open class and encourage other students to disagree if they feel that their classmates have got a match wrong.

Now give the groups up to ten minutes to write up their lists of advantages and disadvantages. Should you wish to shorten this stage, you may choose to assign each group a single production method to work on. Ensure that each method is being discussed by at least one group. Encourage discussion of the groups' ideas in open class. If you asked groups to concentrate on one production method, allow a few more minutes now for students to take a note of the advantages and disadvantages of the production methods they didn't work on.

A 3
B 1
C 2

# 6 Products and production

## Listening: Production and its management

**1** Tell your students that they are going to be introduced to key vocabulary which will come up in the listening exercise. Give them a few minutes to carry out the matching on their own before checking answers in open class.

> 1 e, 2 a, 3 d, 4 b, 5 c

**2** Given the length of the listening – and the complexity of some of the issues discussed in it – prepare yourself in advance of your class for the discussion which will take place by reading the audioscript on pages 148–149.

Prepare students for the listening by getting them to look at the questions and discussing what they already know about the issues. Emphasize that in the course of the listening they should take notes in answer to the questions.

When the listening is over, invite your students to go over their notes for a few moments and note down points that they didn't have time to elaborate upon. Collect answers in open class and encourage students to supplement each others' answers with additional information that they may have missed.

> 1 Production is important for the economy because it is the value created by it upon which an economy's wealth is based. Other activities such as IT and marketing play only a subsidiary role to the real business of creating value which is the role of production.
> 2 Lean manufacturing, which evolved out of approaches to production adopted by *Toyota*, is a system which reduces lead times, boosts efficiency and quality by reducing waste in the manufacturing process. It is a new approach to management – a change in behavior rather than in technology.
> 3 Waste is defined as activities which do not add value to production.
> 4 It has been difficult to implement lean production in a Western context partly as a result of a misinterpretation of the term: Western companies tended to see it as a recipe for making their workforces lean and shedding jobs. Lean production implies a process-driven focus which Western companies have found difficult to achieve.
> 5 Workers need to be trained to identify and solve problems as well as communicate effectively and work successfully within teams. They also have to have knowledge of different stages of production in order that they can be flexibly redeployed.
> 6 This might happen because the companies in question have not found it possible to shift their thinking from a "hire and fire" mentality to one where they invest in staff development and the improvement of processes.

**3** Ask your students to read the questions before playing the CD track again. Collect answers in open class.

> 1 inventory waste, waste from product defects, over-production waste, waste of motion, processing waste, waiting waste, transportation waste
> 2 The Japanese approach to improving results is to focus on improving processes, machinery and investing in the workforce.
> 3 The challenges in production – and management – are posed by the need for constant adaptation to meet the demands of increasingly shorter production cycles and burgeoning information flows, as well as technological developments.

**4** Divide your students into small groups and tell them that they should carry out this research as homework.

You may choose to direct your students' internet research. For instance, encourage them to search specific websites, such as http://www.themanufacturer.com/ using keywords such as *waste*.

> 1 Waste occurs in different ways. At the level of inventory, waste comes about when more components than can be used in production are purchased leaving a company with inventory in hand. Waste can also occur if a company invests in large warehousing facilities for components rather than using a JIT approach to inventory.
> If defective products are produced, waste comes about through a company having to repair or replace these. Waste can be generated through over-production, i.e. when a company is left with more products than it can sell: it has allocated production resources and materials for items which customers are not interested in.
> There can also be waste in the manufacturing process itself – or the associated logistical process – where particular parts of the process are not efficient enough leading to bottlenecks and downtime.
> 2 Should a company ignore waste it runs the risk of driving up its costs and thus not being sufficiently competitive. It also risks not being able to respond swiftly enough to changes brought about by shifts in market demand or technological developments.

Begin the next class by asking the groups to summarize the results of their investigations.

## Products and production 6

### Reading: Birth of the cool

**1** Point out the importance of the vocabulary here for the students' understanding of the reading they are about to do and give them a couple of minutes to work with the person next to them to match the terms to the photographs. Confirm the correct answers in open class.

> A nuts and bolts  D assembly line
> B mold  E conveyor belt
> C barcode decal

**2** Ask your students if any of them have ever worked in factories. What are their impressions of factory work? Note their ideas on the board in the form of keywords. You might also extend this by asking your students about the role of factory work in contemporary society: does it employ as many people as it did in the past and provide the "job for life" model of employment? Your students should now read the short paragraph. Ask them if the picture of factory work sketched here resembles their own view.

**3** Ask the students to read the article: their initial task is to establish if the workers described have a similar experience of factory work to that of the short paragraph's author. Encourage the students to skim read the article. It describes a production process which is largely automated; workers don't crop up in it until around half way through (though you shouldn't tell them this), so much of its content has no bearing on the question they are addressing. Tell them that they should attempt to gain an impression of what the article says without seeking explanation of any unknown vocabulary. You may decide to encourage your students further to skim read by setting a time limit: give them no more than five minutes to complete their reading.

When the students have finished reading, allow some minutes for open discussion about the similarities between the experience of the worker who wrote the short paragraph and those described in the article. Try to draw as many students as possible into the discussion and encourage them to back up their arguments with evidence from the article.

**4** Your students should then complete the flow chart. Point out that the goal of the exercise is to provide the information in summary form. Students should pay particular attention to identifying the right verbs to use in their summaries.

Check answers by asking one student or pair to write their summary of the first step on the board before asking other students to comment upon it and make suggestions for additions. Ask a different student to do the same with the second step and so on.

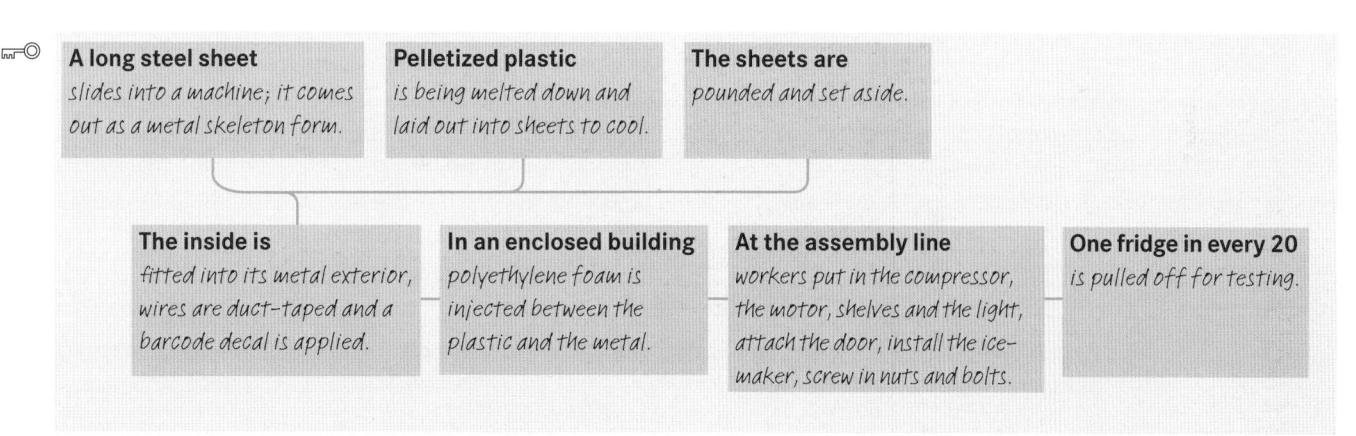

> **A long steel sheet** slides into a machine; it comes out as a metal skeleton form.
>
> **Pelletized plastic** is being melted down and laid out into sheets to cool.
>
> **The sheets are** pounded and set aside.
>
> **The inside is** fitted into its metal exterior, wires are duct-taped and a barcode decal is applied.
>
> **In an enclosed building** polyethylene foam is injected between the plastic and the metal.
>
> **At the assembly line** workers put in the compressor, the motor, shelves and the light, attach the door, install the ice-maker, screw in nuts and bolts.
>
> **One fridge in every 20** is pulled off for testing.

**5** You might choose to liven up the activity by dividing your students into small groups and turning this exercise into a quiz. Ensure that the students understand that only one of the verbs fits in each case and that some of the verbs will have to change their form.

Read out the first sentence - without, of course, filling in the gap - then pause to let the groups decide which verb fits. Award a point for the correct choice of verb and a further point for the correct manipulation of form. If a group answers incorrectly on either account, invite the other groups to put up their hands quickly for a chance to answer and earn further points. Continue in this manner until all the gaps have been completed and declare the group with the most points the winner.

> 1 The apartment <u>contains</u> a mini-kitchen facility and an en-suite shower/WC.
> 2 The home improvement guide shows you how to <u>attach</u> the shelves to the wall.
> 3 The car mechanic advised me to <u>install</u> new cables and a new battery in my van.
> 4 Containers are stowed by <u>stacking</u> them on top of each other to make full use of the loading capacity.
> 5 By <u>applying</u> a thin layer of car wax on a regular basis, you can protect your car from UV rays and dirt.

# 6 Products and production

## Manufacturing keywords board game

Help your students to consolidate key manufacturing terminology from the Course Book unit by getting them to play this board game. You will need one board game for each pair of students. Each pair will need three coins to play: two of these are playing pieces; one will be used in place of a die (heads = move one space; tails = move two spaces. 'Tails' is the side of the coin that shows its value.).

The first player tosses the coin, moves the appropriate number of spaces and completes the task in the square. Regardless of whether they get this right or wrong, they then remain on the square while the other player takes their turn. The first player to reach the last square wins.

Place a copy of the answer key at the front of the classroom for students to consult.

Key:
1. A series of operations performed to shape, form or improve material to make it ready for assembly.
2. lead
3. An approach to production which focuses on eliminating waste from the production process with a view to boosting quality and cutting costs.
4. workforce
6. defect
7. An approach to manufacturing where the quantities of goods produced are directly determined by customer demand.
9. shop floor
10. A series of operations performed to make a finished product.
12. Similar to make-to-order production, this approach synchronizes final processing and delivery doing away with the final parts store. Final processing is activated as orders from customers come in.
13. Inventory waste, waste from product defects, overproduction waste, waste of motion, processing waste, waiting waste, transportation waste
15. A conventional approach to production where production outputs are determined by expectations and projections.
17. inventory
18. assembly

## Discussion: Can business expertise of the 20th century still be applied today?

Ask your students to explain what they know about Henry Ford and his approach to manufacturing. Elicit from the class that Ford was one of the industrialists behind the development of conveyor belt production lines and that his emphasis on mass production and mass standardization resulted in cars which were cheap enough to be sold in a mass market. This was in contrast to other car manufacturers who regarded their product as being suitable only for "luxury" markets. Round off by either eliciting from or pointing out to your students that Ford's model of production held sway for much of the 20th century. Other systems of production in which the emphasis has been on using the methods of mass-production to address demand in niche markets have enjoyed popularity since the 1980s.

Now split your students into groups setting them the task of deciding in which industries the "Fordist" approach might still be applied and in which the newer ideas of "mass-customization" may be more suitable. Prompt their thinking by suggesting they first take the manufacture of home electronics goods into consideration. Give the groups ten minutes for their discussions before bringing the class back together.

If you want to read more about the issue of production, you can search for "Fordism and Post Fordism" on the internet.

### Business Skills

## Presentations: Presenting a product

1. Focus the students' thinking by asking the class to brainstorm the things needed to make use of a computer. Prompt with an example, such as electricity. Then ask what might be lacking in a remote location in Africa. Write the students' suggestions on the board: when you feel that the lists are long enough, encourage the students to decide what attributes a computer designed for such an environment might have and write their ideas on the board.

2. Point out to the students that they are to listen only for the answers to the four questions.

3. Draw the students' attention to the product description mind map giving them a few moments to consider the categories on it. Explain that as they listen to the presentation a second time, they are to note the appropriate information into the mind map. Write the correct answers on the board so that students can check the spelling.

# Products and production 6

## 1

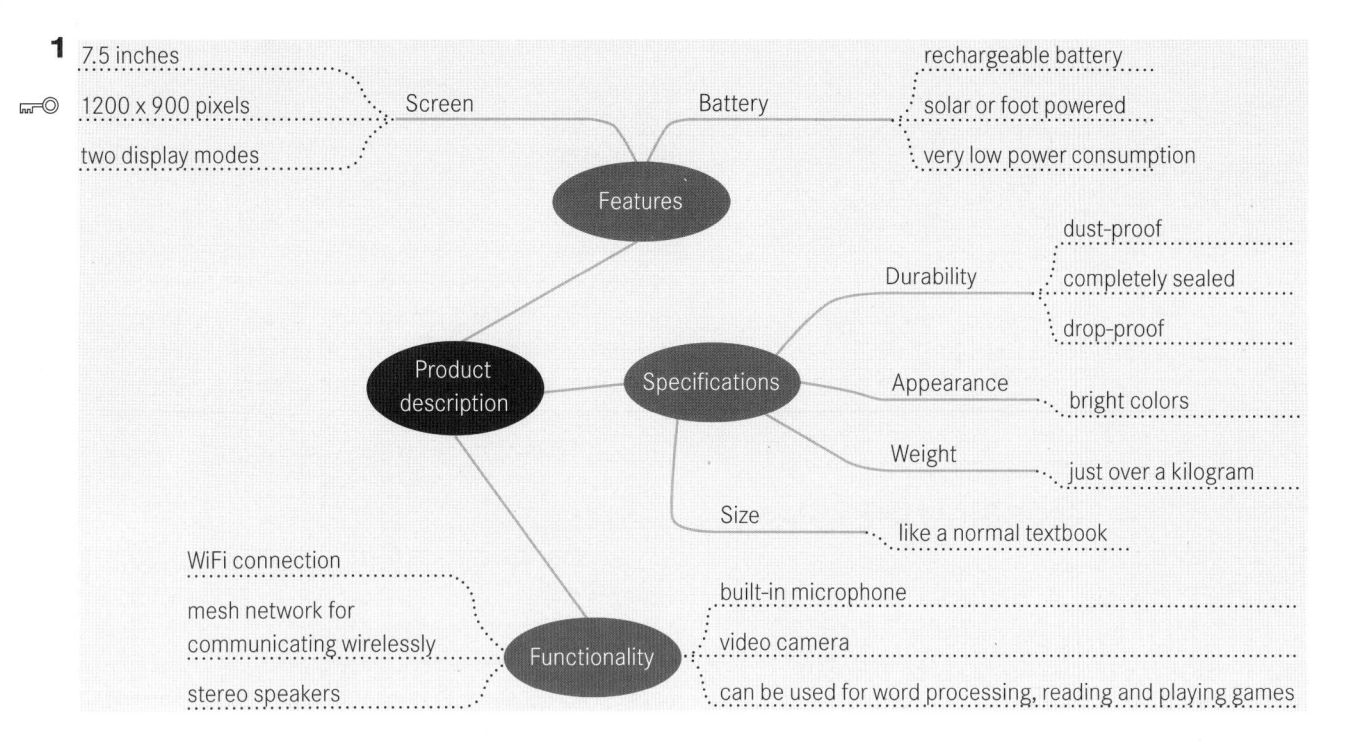

**Features**
- Screen: 7.5 inches; 1200 x 900 pixels; two display modes
- Battery: rechargeable battery; solar or foot powered; very low power consumption

**Specifications**
- Durability: dust-proof; completely sealed; drop-proof
- Appearance: bright colors
- Weight: just over a kilogram
- Size: like a normal textbook

**Functionality**
- WiFi connection
- mesh network for communicating wirelessly
- stereo speakers
- built-in microphone
- video camera
- can be used for word processing, reading and playing games

## Presentations: Describing a product

Encourage the pairs to structure their exchange of information by sketching a three-column table on the board: head the middle and right-hand column *Kindle* and *Sony* and write the appropriate categories down the left-hand column; *readability, data input, storage capacity, size, weight* and *price*.

|  | Kindle | Sony |
|---|---|---|
| readability | | |
| data input | | |
| storage capacity | | |
| size | | |
| weight | | |
| price | | |

The pairs should make one copy of this table to use between them when exchanging specifications. While the first student describes the features of their e-reader, the second student listens and notes the features in the appropriate place on the table. The students then change roles and the table changes hands to be filled in by the other student. Remind your students that they can also put questions to each other to draw out further comparative information about the product. Finally, before they carry out the information swap, remind the students of the language for describing technical specifications which they encountered in the listening. Students should try to use at least four of these phrases while making their description. The pairs should conclude their discussion by saying which e-reader they would personally prefer to use and why.

Round up the activity by bringing the class back together and asking students at random to comment upon whether they personally would use an e-reader.

## Writing: Product descriptions

**1** Ask your students to compare the specification and functionality sheet with the product description on page 60. Their task will be to identify which features detailed on the specification sheet are given particular prominence in the description on the company's website. These features will inevitably be the product's USPs. Confirm the correct answers in open class.

**2** Prompt your students' thinking by asking them to explore the order the information is presented in. They should also focus on the kind of descriptive language which is used to animate the product description. Give the students ten minutes to discuss the product description before bringing the class back together and encouraging discussion about how the text effectively "packages" its message.

> The product description engages readers by means of a two-pronged strategy. Firstly, what might otherwise be a dull list of technical specifications is enlivened through the use of adverbs and adjectives which make the product sound more appealing, i.e. the device is *ultra-thin* and *powerful*. Secondly,

51

# 6 Products and production

the readers' attention is repeatedly drawn to the practical benefits that these specifications would imply for them as users of the device: it makes note taking *quick and easy* and makes reading *effortless*. Thus, an emotional appeal – It will make your life easier – is made to readers of the product description.

**3** Prepare your students for their writing task, which should be carried out as homework, by reminding them of the importance of the structure of their product description and the kind of descriptive language used in it to capture the interest of potential customers. Additionally, draw your students' attention to the language box at the bottom of page 60 encouraging them to use as many of the phrases as they can in their product descriptions.

Your students should give you their product descriptions to you sufficiently in advance of the next class to allow you to return them with your comments before the class. Focus your comments on the use students have made of descriptive language as well as the structure of their texts.

## Company Case: **Crossing borders**

Begin by setting the scene for your students. Point out that the dilemma presented in the case study is realistic and is faced, by manufacturers who are constantly confronted with the tempting possibility of relocating production to lower-waged countries. Before students read the text, ask them to brainstorm lists of the advantages and disadvantages to companies of relocating their production bases: while a lower wage bill and increased worker flexibility are generally the advantages of such relocations, companies may have to reckon with training the new workforce as well as the blow to their public relations caused by factory closures.

Ask students to read the case study, then, in their groups, consider the options open to the company. They should create a list of pros and cons for each option in order to help them assess which would best serve the company's interests.

Prompt their thinking further by asking students to what extent moving to Mexico may deplete the company's PR in the U.S. Additionally, ask them if negotiating a pay cut with the unions is a viable option. Even if the company can secure a cut in wages, it will not succeed in reducing pay to Mexican levels: however, the pay cut is sure to cause disgruntlement among the workforce which might affect productivity. Finally, encourage the students to consider further options for cutting costs which would make relocation unnecessary.

Encourage your students to draft their final recommendations in presentation form with a clear introduction, main body of argument and conclusion. Allow up to 20 minutes for this.

Bring the class back together asking each group in turn to make their presentations.

# Over to you

## Web research: The ideal business location?

Encourage students to complete the task by making clear that you are allotting part of the next class to reviewing and discussing the results of their research.

## Writing: Responding to a company's outsourcing plan

Encourage your students to complete the writing by inviting them to give their work to you for your comments. Should you feel that three pieces of writing are too much for each student, introduce a division of labor into the task allocating each student one piece of writing. You should, of course, ensure that each of the three tasks is being covered by at least one student.

# 7 Marketing communications

## Self Study

**Vocabulary**
- The word family *advertis-*
- Collocations: running an advertising campaign
- How good is your marketing knowledge?

**Grammar**
- Counting on your grammar: Count and non-count nouns
- Quantifiers: *some*, *a lot of* or *hardly any* marketing?
- Some more quantifiers

**Skills**
- Opening and closing a presentation
- Guiding the listener through a presentation
- Creating slides

**Reading**
- Dealing with unfamiliar words
- Recognizing text organization

**Video**
- How to start a presentation
- Preparing a presentation
- What's it about?
- Strategies for handling difficult questions
- What makes a convincing presentation?

## At a glance

This unit will equip your students with the language of the important marketing processes which companies have to carry out in order to remain competitive. The unit covers the multifaceted tasks performed by marketing professionals from the initial market research stage through to the positioning of marketing messages by means of advertising and other modern marketing communications strategies.

The unit ensures that students will be up-to-speed with the fundamental definitions of marketing thinking and will be in a position to describe concepts such as the **marketing mix** and **niche marketing**. Students will also be in a position to talk about contemporary concepts in marketing such as **focus group research** and **mass customization**.

Unit 7 reflects recent developments in marketing communications more thoroughly by examining strategies such as **viral marketing**, **ambush marketing** and **guerrilla marketing**, and affords students the opportunity to think about the applicability of these in relation to a diverse range of products. It also investigates the growing tendency in marketing communications to target messages at clearly defined target groups through an examination of **ethnic marketing**.

The unit is complemented by the *Business Skills* section's focus on presentations. Good presentation skills will be of general importance to your students. However, they are particularly applicable to marketing, the key task of which is the clear presentation of products and concepts to potential customers.

For a large number of short articles on a variety of marketing topics see:
http://marketing.about.com/

For a wide range of tutorial texts covering all aspects of the marketing process see:
http://managementhelp.org/mrktng/mrktng.htm

## Warm-up

As an alternative to instructing your students to answer the multiple choice questions on their own, turn this activity into a classroom quiz. Split your class into teams and be prepared to play the role of the quiz master. Read out the questions and answers with a slightly dramatic TV-style voice. Give team members a moment to confer after each question. To indicate that they are ready to answer the team members should spring to their feet. The first team to do so – and answer correctly – wins a point. The team with the most points at the end wins.
You may have to assist your students in understanding some of the lexis from the questionnaire, in particular, *primary data*, *qualitative data* and *quantitative data* may require some explanation. Explain the first term by telling your students that data from published sources such as magazines or the internet is referred to as *secondary data*: this should help students to draw their own conclusions as to the definition of *primary data*. Assist your students with *quantitative data* and *qualitative data* by pointing out that one refers to data that will be quantified for analysis and the other to the quality of the data that has been collected. Students should draw their own conclusions as to which is which but ensure that they understand the lexis once the quiz is over.
After completing the quiz, allow your students a few moments to add up their scores and read the comments about their performance in the bottom left-hand corner of the page.

# 7 Marketing communications

The students should remain in their groups to discuss the question at the bottom of page 64. If they have answered the questions on their own, put them into groups for the discussion. You may want to pose an additional question: what type of marketing strategies tend to have the biggest influence on your students as individuals? Prompt the students by describing the ways you have been influenced by marketing. After allowing five minutes for their discussion, ask your students to call out their ideas and write them on the board assisting with reformulation where necessary.

## Listening: Passing the buck

**1** Before playing the listening, prepare your students for it by drawing their attention to the photograph and the job titles. Ask them to spend two minutes with the person sitting next to them discussing what they think each person's job involves. Bring the class back together, get the students to call out their ideas and write these on the board.

> **Vice-president of Marketing:** oversees all the marketing activities of the company from market research, developing marketing plans to delivering selling messages in the marketplace, reports on the company's marketing activities to the board of directors
>
> **PR and Advertising manager:** responsible for overseeing the design, placement and buying and evaluation of advertising, as well as public relations activities, such as special sponsored events and press relations
>
> **Market Research manager:** in charge of designing, conducting and evaluating market research, which is usually conducted through in-depth interviews, surveys, market analyses, and experiments

Ask your students to spend a moment reading the three questions. They should then spend a moment to speculate about possible reasons for the company's problems. Should they find it difficult to come up with ideas, prompt your students with a couple of suggestions. The company may, for instance, have advertised in the wrong places or the advertising budget may not have been large enough.

Now play the listening, asking students to keep the three questions and their speculations in mind. Confirm the correct answers after the listening.

> - The sales figures have not risen as expected.
> - The expensive advertising campaign was not reaching the target group.
> - They decide to invite a consultant over to talk about alternative advertising methods.

**2** Before playing the listening again, ask the students to work individually for two minutes and try to complete the gaps from memory. Take the pressure out of this by pointing out that you don't expect them to remember all of the terms used and they may well only remember one or two. Students then listen again, fill in the remaining gaps and check if their memories served them correctly.

> 1 Wait a minute, we got the <u>target group</u> right.
> 2 *CoolFit* is the first brand of jeans to use <u>mass customization</u>.
> 3 We used <u>surveys</u> and <u>focus groups</u> until we were sure we had an unbeatable <u>feature</u> – guaranteed fit.
> 4 We ran a fantastic <u>advertising campaign</u> on <u>prime-time</u> television coast to coast.
> 5 We backed this up with <u>billboards</u> and <u>celebrity endorsements</u>.
> 6 You're paid to know that this age group doesn't watch <u>commercials</u> anymore. In fact, they reject <u>advertising hype</u>.

You may choose to explore the language of the listening further. Ask your students to evaluate the tone of the conversation. Turn your students' attention to the audioscript on pages 149–150 setting them the task of identifying the rather direct phrases used by the participants. Confirm the answers by writing them on the board and make sure your students understand what they mean. Round off the activity by pointing out that such phrases, though entirely authentic, may cause offence and should be handled with care.

> - Somebody hasn't been doing their homework.
> - So you've just passed the buck.
> - Spare me the details.
> - You're paid to know that …
> - Well, you can't have your cake and eat it too.

## Reading: Alternative methods of marketing

**1** Write the five marketing terms on the board, ask students to close their books and give them two minutes to pool their knowledge of the terms before discussing the terms with the whole class. Ask your students to cite any real-life examples of the approaches to advertising that they may know of prompting them to comment on which campaign they found most compelling.

54

# Marketing communications 7

**2** You may consider animating this exercise further by printing the five definitions and examples onto strips of paper for your students to match. Allowing students to shuffle definitions and examples around in front of them may help some of them to complete the matching more successfully.

Then invite questions about unknown vocabulary and be prepared to define *launch*, *appeal*, *savvy*, *reluctant* and *subscriber*.

If your students have not already read the definitions on the left-hand side of the page, invite them to do so now in order to establish if the definitions they offered earlier can be supplemented with additional information. Deal with unknown vocabulary after collecting any additional information the students have gleaned from their reading and be prepared to offer definitions of *incentive*, *exposure*, *deceptive* and *embedded*.

🔑
| | | |
|---|---|---|
| Guerrilla marketing: | D | *Sony Ericsson* |
| Viral marketing: | C | *Hotmail* |
| Word-of-mouth: | A | *Nintendo of America Inc.* |
| Ambush marketing: | E | *Nike* |
| Advergaming: | B | *Oreo Cookies* |

Round off this exercise by returning briefly to the discussion during step 1. If your students were not in a position to define some of the terms and cite examples of them at this stage, ask them to think of examples now, getting them to comment on which campaign they personally found most effective and describe the strategy which underpinned it.

**10C** Word power – Collocation matching cards

> This photocopiable activity will help you to exploit the reading texts on page 66 further. After students have completed the reading tasks, spend a few moments refreshing their memories about collocations and their value. Explain that they are going to complete a card-matching exercise featuring key collocations from the texts.

> Pair off your students giving each pair a cut-up and shuffled set of collocation cards which they should spread out on the table in front of them. Tell them that they have three minutes to match the cards forming the collocations used in the texts. When they have completed this matching, ask students to scan the texts again to confirm their answers.

> Round off the activity by pointing out that several other frequently-used two-word phrases arise from the words in the set. Some students may have already identified these in the course of matching the cards. Allow your students a further three minutes to identify other collocations which they may know.

🔑 Other possible collocations:
sporting environment, sponsorship strategy, sponsorship budget, official events, promotional events, promotional budget, low fees, advertising budget, promotion strategy, promotion budget

**3** Pair off your students asking them to decide which of the five approaches to marketing could be used to promote the products listed. Then allow a few more minutes for students to discuss which strategies they matched to which products. Complete this stage by pointing out which products from the list would probably best be marketed using more conventional means.

Extend this activity by asking each pair to choose one of the products which might be effectively marketed using the five methods. The pairs should spend five minutes sketching out a marketing strategy for the product featuring one or more of the marketing strategies with the aim of giving a one-minute presentation of their strategy to their classmates. The short presentations complete, congratulate your students on their innovative approach to marketing.

Your students should remain in their pairs for the following exercise.

## Role-play: Bringing your marketing knowledge into play

**1** Ask the students to brainstorm all the conventional means of marketing that they can think of and write their list of ideas on the board.

Tell the students that their task is now to concentrate on how the product will be advertised. You could also increase the challenge by asking students to decide which proportion of an advertising budget they would suggest for each method of advertising.

Draw the students' attention to the *Developing ideas* language box and tell them that they should each attempt to use three phrases from the box in the course of their discussion. Now set the students loose on their task, reminding them that there are no right or wrong answers, but that they should prepare arguments to justify their choices. Give the pairs about ten minutes to develop their marketing plans as well as the arguments in its favor. While they are doing so, circulate and be prepared to help with additional suggestions and formulation.

55

# 7 Marketing communications

**2** Pair off your students afresh making sure that those who will role-play the *CoolFit* Marketing director should ask as many probing questions about the promotion campaign being presented to them as possible. The other students should be prepared to put all their weight behind selling the plan.

You may wish to give the students role-playing the Marketing director a chance to pitch their own marketing plan which will require that you once again put your class into new pairs. In order to prevent these two run-throughs of the role-play taking up too much time, put a time cap of ten or a maximum of 15 minutes on each role-play.

Listen in on the role-plays as the students are performing them. To round off, pair up the student who you think pitched most effectively with the student who made the best job of the marketing director role and ask them to perform the role-play in front of the class.

## Diversity: Ethnic marketing

If you have several students from different ethnic backgrounds, ensure that they are spread throughout the groups so that the views of people of diverse ethnicity are represented in all the group discussions. However, do this with sensitivity and be aware that some people may not enjoy being "singled out" due to their ethnicity – avoid putting people "on the spot".

After ten minutes of discussion – you can move from group to group contributing for a short while as you see fit – bring the class back together and invite volunteers from each group to summarize their discussions. Pay particular attention to question 4, writing a list of the students' suggestions on the board. The list might include ideas, such as using different languages to reach various target groups in ethnically segmented markets, featuring photographs of people from different ethnic groups in ads. Students might also list sensitivity to cultural issues or the use of advertising media directed to members of specific ethnic groups.

## Business Skills

## Presentations: Reaching your audience

**1** Split the students into small groups asking them to think of terrible presentations they've experienced and to analyze what went wrong. Ask students to draw up a list of mistakes that can have negative effects on presentations. Draw their attention to the cartoon asking them to think about what might be going wrong during the presentation depicted in it. After around five minutes, bring the class back together and ask students to call out their ideas which you should write up on the board. Their list may be a long one and might include the following points:

- a presentation can be too long
- its aims and the structure of the presentation can be unclear
- too much irrelevant information
- the presenter might speak unclearly, too fast or simply read the slides
- there are too many visuals to consider while listening
- the presenter's nervous hand gestures distract attention
- the presenter does not handle questions well in the course of the presentation allowing them to break up the flow

### Video: An internship abroad: Presentation

Consolidate what the students have covered so far by referring to the video. Split your viewing of it into two stages: first, the rehearsal scene at the beginning and then the presentation itself.

Start by giving your students the task of finding out which rules about giving presentations Harold states and whether he himself sticks to these rules.

You may wish to encourage your students to draw out the presentation language used by Harold. In order to do this, ask the following questions before playing the scene again.

1. What does he say to welcome his audience?
2. What does he say in order to introduce the structure of his presentation?
3. How does he structure his presentation overview?

1. Good afternoon ladies and gentlemen. First of all, let me say how nice it is to see you all here at *Exhilarate* today.
2. Let me give you an idea of what I'm going to be talking about.
3. First we'll look at the objectives of the event. Then, I'll outline the marketing campaign and finally I'll give a quick overview of the expected return on investment.

# Marketing communications 7

Now ask students to watch Rebecca's presentation to assess how well she performs. Prompt students to take notes of any aspects of her style which they liked. Again, ask them to call out their suggestions after viewing and write these up.

> - She appears confident and relaxed.
> - Her pace is good – not too fast and not too slow.
> - Her manner is pleasant and friendly.
> - She speaks very clearly.

Stop the video clip before Daumier's final assessment of Rebecca's presentation and ask the students whether they think Rebecca made any mistakes during her presentation and prompt students to volunteer their suggestions.

> Rebecca is rather static – she remains seated and makes little use of her hands. She also mistakenly refers to how dangerous ice climbing is.

Before turning back to the Course Book and the mind map on page 68, ask the students to recall Harold's rehearsal of his presentation in front of Rebecca: which elements from the introduction of a presentation were mentioned. Get the students to call out what they remember and write up their suggestions.

**2** Now ask the students to close their Course Books so that they cannot refer to the mind map and give the groups a further three minutes or so to consider what the beginning of a presentation should include. Again, consolidate their ideas on the board without at this stage commenting on them. The list should include:

- presenters should introduce themselves and greet the audience
- there should be an overview of what the presentation will include and its overall structure as well as an indication of the importance of what is going to be argued
- presenters should indicate how long the presentation will take and say whether questions will be accepted during the presentation or once it is over

Ask your students to open their Course Books at page 68 and look at the mind map.

Then play track 04 so students can judge if Bob Spencer has conformed to the mind map in his introduction.

> Except for stating the importance of what he is going to say, Bob covers all the points on the mind map.

Play the track again so that students can note the phrases that Spencer uses in his introduction. If you feel that some of your students might find this difficult and want to avoid a third run-through of the CD track, you might consider pausing the CD after each utterance so that students can note them down.

### Presentation workout

> Tell your students they are going to get some additional practice in presentation introductions. Pair them off giving each pair a cut-up presentation introduction. Give them four minutes to sort it into logical order. Note that while the position of the majority of text blocks is fixed within the structure of the introduction, a few text blocks could logically be used at various points.
>
> Now give out the *Student A* and *Student B* role cards to each pair. The students should agree who will work with which card and use the information on their cards to prepare the introduction to a presentation which they will deliver to their partners. Tell the students that they can select "signposting" phrases from the introduction on the photocopiable and from Bob Spencer's introduction in the Course Book.
>
> Allow your students enough time to prepare but set a time limit of ten minutes. Circulate during the preparation stage and offer assistance.
>
> The students should now deliver their introductions to their partners. While they are doing so, listen in on individual students and take note of mistakes or particularly successful elements of their introductions for feeding back at the end.
>
> Round off by asking two or three students to deliver their introductions to the class and don't forget to congratulate your students on their efforts.

**3** Before playing the CD, give your students a few moments to consider questions one and two. Tell them to keep these in mind as they listen and take notes.

> 1 The purpose of the campaign is to get everybody in the target group talking about the clever advertising and, consequently, about *CoolFit* jeans.
> 2 *Step 1:* Produce three amateurish video clips.
> *Step 2:* Distribute the clips to young adults on the internet.
> *Step 3:* Wait for a month for the video clips to be distributed virally on the internet and for the buzz to build up.
> *Step 4:* Run TV and radio ads and employ buzz agents to reveal the true nature of the video clips.

# 7 Marketing communications

Now ask the students to work with the person sitting next to them on the question of whether they think the *Buzz World* strategy will work. Add a further element to their task by asking them to consider not only whether the proposal would work but also why. After a few minutes, ask which students are convinced by the proposal and which aren't forming them into two groups according to their opinions. Draw a line down the center of the board, head up the two resulting columns *Convinced – why?* and *Unconvinced – why?* and ask the members of the two groups to work together on either side of the board writing up bullet points which summarize why they think the proposal will or will not work. When they have completed this, ask a volunteer from each group to present their bullet points to the class. Afterwards, ask for elaboration regarding any points which you find are too briefly stated or are of particular interest. Round off by asking if any of the students have changed their opinion due to the discussion.

## Presentations: **Preparing slides**

**1** The purpose of this exercise is to ensure that your students understand the five vocabulary items in advance of listening to Prof Ainsley Barnes' talk. Allow the students a few minutes to complete it, then check their answers in open class.
   1. Their relationship used to be friendly, but now there is a lot of <u>hostility</u> between the CEO and the CFO.
   2. TV advertising rates are generally quoted per 30-second time <u>slot</u>.
   3. A <u>drawback</u> of television advertising is that viewers tend to switch channels during a commercial.
   4. Some people think that <u>clutter</u> on a desk is a sign of genius.
   5. Our own sales methods haven't worked. We need a completely new <u>appearance</u>.

**2** Refer to exercise 1 again and ensure that your students understand that they are to consider which of the three slides would best support Prof Barnes' lecture on *Forms of Advertising*.

Before playing the lecture, point out to your students that their task is to get an overview of what it contains rather than to understand what Barnes argues word for word. Ask them to

## Writing: **Presentation slides**

Writing the following headlines on the board:

   a  Online advertising – more modern than advertising on T.V.
   b  Living in the age of online advertising
   c  The advantages of online advertising – low cost and easy to measure results

Give your students a moment to read these, then ask them to read the text and decide which headline best summarizes it. Point out that they should scan the text quickly ignoring words they don't know in order to get a brief overview. After inviting

**4** Before playing the CD, ensure that your students understand that they are to note what Spencer says about the effectiveness, costs, risks and success of what his agency is proposing. Check the students' answers in open class.

Now ask the class to consider the purpose of this final part of the presentation. Ask your students to write their ideas on the board. When you feel that they can make no further suggestions confirm that the purpose of this section is to:

- sell the proposal
- show that the chances of success are high
- point that the associated risks and costs are low
- summarize the key idea of the presentation
- thank the audience
- invite questions

relax while they are listening and ignore elements which they do not understand. After listening, ask the students to evaluate each slide in turn.

   1  contains too much information, confusing due to different fonts and sizes
   2  contains too little information

Ask your students to close their Course Books and return to their small groups: on this occasion their task is to come up with a list of *do's* and *don't's* about writing presentation slides. Give them several minutes to complete this, casting an eye over their work as they do so. When you feel that they have noted everything they can think of, ask them to open their Course Books on page 70 and compare their lists of *do's* and *don't's* with those that appear in the top left-hand corner of the page. Ask several students to comment upon whether their list contained significant differences to that in the Course Book. Conclude by pointing out that the list of *do's* and *don't's* on page 70 is a sound summary of how to go about writing presentation slides.

suggestions from a few students as to the best headline, confirm that headline c fits the bill best.

Tell your students that their next task is to write a presentation slide summarizing the text about online advertising. Invite them to read the text again in more detail and ask questions at this stage about any vocabulary they don't understand. Ask two or three students to state the argument of the text. Having confirmed that the students understand the text and their task, give them between five and ten minutes to create their

# Marketing communications 7

slides. Additionally, you could ask your students to think of a graphic or photograph which could be used on the slide to illustrate their argument. Set them this task for homework: at the next class they should hand in their illustrated slide for you to comment upon.

Correct the slides and offer suggestions for improvements before returning them to the students at the next class.

The key criteria for assessing the slides will be to evaluate how successfully each student has identified the key information in the text and conformed to the *do's* and *don't's* list.

> **Benefits of online advertising:**
> - interactivity
> - voluntary transactions
> - measurable actions
> - easy to change and up-date
> - low cost

## Presentations: **Icebreakers**

**1** Ask your students to identify the two attention-grabbing techniques being used and what the intended effects of the two examples from the Course Book might have been.

The intended effect of the *Microsoft©* slide is clearly to raise a smile from an audience. Who would have thought that the company founded in a garage in 1975 by the small team of computer "geeks" would go on to be the largest computer company in the world? Point out, however, that while humor can be a good means of engaging an audience's attention, students should take care to ensure that the humor they deploy is not going to offend anyone, especially when presenting to people from other cultures.

> **Example 1:** *showing a picture plus rhetorical question*
> The intended effect here may have been to point out to the audience in a humorous way that first impressions may indeed be misleading.
> **Example 2:** *offering a surprising fact*
> The intended effect here may have been to underline the difficulty of reaching consumers through conventional means of advertising given how many marketing messages they are confronted with on a daily basis.

**2** Ask your students to work with their partners to brainstorm a list of possible icebreakers. Introduce an element of competition by telling your students that this is a race to see which pair can come up with the longest list. Set them a maximum of five minutes for the task, then bring the class back together. Ask each pair to read out their list and write the examples which you feel to be most useful on the board. Be wary of dismissing ideas out of hand – even if they are a touch outlandish – and congratulate the winning pair. Now turn your attention to the list on the board getting students to flesh out the ideas with examples where necessary.

> The list might include showing a short video clip, playing a song, telling a joke, asking a rhetorical question, telling a story that leads into the theme of the presentation and asking a member of the audience to comment on something or answer a question.

## Company Case: **Ökobrause**

### Background

This case study reflects the challenges that companies with brands that are successful in a domestic market face when they try to market their products elsewhere. While a given branding and marketing strategy may work extremely well in one marketplace, when companies look elsewhere to boost their sales they may have to adopt entirely different approaches. This might include choosing different types of advertising and other promotional activities as well as using different distribution channels.

Prepare your students for the case study by asking them if they know of any organic soft drinks. Ask them what sort of branding these drinks adopt. What are their *unique selling propositions* (USPs) which set them apart from other soft drinks on the market? What type of consumers do the students think the drinks are aimed at? Collect their ideas on the board.

Now split your students into groups of three and tell them that they are going to read about a brand of organic soft drink which is to be launched in the North American market. Ask the students to read the first four bullet points from the task and then to skim read the text to find the answers to the questions. When they have done this, quickly confirm that they have understood the gist of the text by asking them to call out the answers.

Now ask them to work in their groups and read the text again more thoroughly. Their task is to come up with a marketing

59

# 7 Marketing communications

strategy for the launch of *Ökobrause* on the U.S. market and to write presentation slides which reflect this.

Give the students twenty minutes to discuss their marketing strategies and write their slides during which you should circulate and offer assistance with formulation. Now bring the students back together for their presentations. If the students have written their slides on paper, you should quickly photocopy one set of these slides for each of the other groups. Give each group a maximum of three minutes to present the results of their discussion and the slides. At the end of each presentation, ask the other students to comment on the slides: how successfully do they capture the presentation's argument without being overburdened with too much information?

After the presentations, congratulate your students on their efforts and round off the activity by asking the students to think about which group presented the most convincing marketing strategy for *Ökobrause* and say why.

## Over to you

### Presentations: Creating slides

Tell your students that they can practice writing presentation slides further by reading the audioscript of the presentation and writing slides for it. Invite them to email their slides to you for your comments. Be sure to either bring their slides to the next class or email them back to your students.

### Web research: Ökobrause

If you want to ensure that your students carry out the web research and also make their task a little more contained, you might consider giving individual students two or three of the questions which they should investigate before the next class. You should, of course, ensure that all of the questions are being covered. You could also give some students the job of finding answers to the questions regarding the British and Australian markets. The results of this research can be compared at the next class.

### Reading: The city that said no to advertising

Entice your students to do the reading and answer the questions by asking them if they think it is possible to reduce the amount of ads that we are all subjected to by passing laws against advertising. Like most of us, many students will probably feel that there is too much advertising. They will probably think, however, that it is unimaginable that advertising can be legislated away. Why not read about a city which attempted to do just that?

**São Paulo Part 1**
1. The city's mayor, Gilberto Kassab.
2. Because he felt that it was "polluting" the city.
3. Small businesses would have to invest a lot of money to remove advertising.
4. The city would lose its income from advertising. Twenty thousand people would lose their jobs.

**São Paulo Part 2**
1. Many people were waiting to remove their signs. Some people had removed signs only to expose unattractive structures.
2. Loss of lettering in colloquial language; loss of sponsorship funding for carnival.
3. Advertising within limits will return. Some forms, such as street furniture, will be tolerated. Only global brands will be able to afford the approved poster-sites.
4. It forces advertising agencies to be more creative. It is helping to reduce pollution.

### Writing: Banning advertising

Encourage your students to write the short essay by telling them that you will be happy to read their work and offer your comments. They can email it to you before the next class. Remind them that essays of this type usually consist of a short introduction in which what will be argued is briefly stated. This is followed by the main body of the argument and rounded off with a concluding section which should briefly summarize what has been argued before offering a conclusion.

You may choose to encourage your students further to do the writing exercise by telling them that it will be the subject of a short discussion at the beginning of the next class.

# 8 Debts, savings and investments

## At a glance

This unit will bring students up to speed with the language needed to discuss the services and facilities offered by banks and other financial services businesses to private customers and businesses as well as focussing on methods of investment and the impact of fiscal policy on the financial environment. In short, the unit provides students with a solid grounding in more than just the fundamentals of financial English. Unit 8 brings home the relevance of the subject by moving quickly to an examination of the dangers to students of relying on bank credit: your class will quickly be in a position to talk about **interest rates**, **current accounts**, **overdrafts**, **grants**, **banking fees** and **budget plans**.

As well as equipping students with a range of vocabulary they will need to discuss investments such as **dividend**, **commission**, **yield**, **maturity** and **performance**, the unit examines investment products and the types of investors these typically suit taking in investment vehicles including **shares**, **bonds**, **futures**, **commercial paper** and **unit trusts**. Thus, the unit familiarizes students with the range of rationales which affect investment decisions.

The *Business Skills* section focuses on negotiating in a financial context acquainting students with and offering them ample opportunity to practice language for structuring negotiations and bringing them to mutually beneficial conclusions.

The unit's *Company Case* gives students the opportunity to put on a banker's hat and consider a tricky investment decision which encompasses not only commercial considerations but also intercultural and ethical aspects.

For background reading about the financial services sector and what makes it tick see:
http://www.moneyweek.com/

For a comprehensive glossary of financial terminology see:
http://www.bloomberg.com/personal-finance

## Self Study

**Vocabulary**
- Know your investment terms
- Do you take your risk small, medium or large?
- Terms of the deal

**Grammar**
- Andy in trouble: what if?
- Know your forms: word families
- Noun/verb collocations: Increase your interest

**Skills**
- Understanding negotiations
- Linking offers to conditions
- Finding the right words: give yourself credit!

**Reading**
- Righting wrongs: reading closely
- Roaring panic: guessing meaning from context

## Warm-up

This exercise offers your students an opportunity to think about the chain reactions which might take place as a result of the developments mentioned in the headlines. As such it is an ideal preparation for the type of thinking they are going to have to do in the course of the unit.

Split them into pairs and demonstrate how you want them to tackle the exercise by completing the first example together with a couple of students you judge have good heads for economics on their shoulders. Write up the results of this on the board in the following way encouraging the groups to use a similar approach when they discuss the other headlines:

"Banks took on too much risk" → near collapse of banking system → economic slow-down and rising unemployment → government bail outs for banks → increased burden on taxpayer → probably negative effect for people in my position

Set the groups loose on the other headlines giving them 10 minutes to discuss and note their probable consequences. Round off by asking different groups to come to the board and write up their "chain reactions". Help with formulation where necessary offering phrases such as *The result of this will be ..., the knock on effect will probably be ..., ... which will in turn lead to ...*

# 8 Debts, savings and investments

## Listening: The debt trap

**1** Your students should remain in their groups for this exercise which you could approach either by asking the groups to brainstorm all six categories of the mind map or setting different groups the task of brainstorming just two or three of the categories. The latter approach will give students more opportunity to think in-depth about specific categories and should lead to more complete results from the class without the brainstorming taking too long.

While the groups are brainstorming and filling in their mind maps, quickly draw the mind map on the board, then circulate listening in on the discussions. When you judge that they have had enough time, bring the students back together, consolidating the results of their discussions by completing the mind map on the board. Note that the mind map reproduced below as an answer key is not definitive: it can be extended with students' ideas.

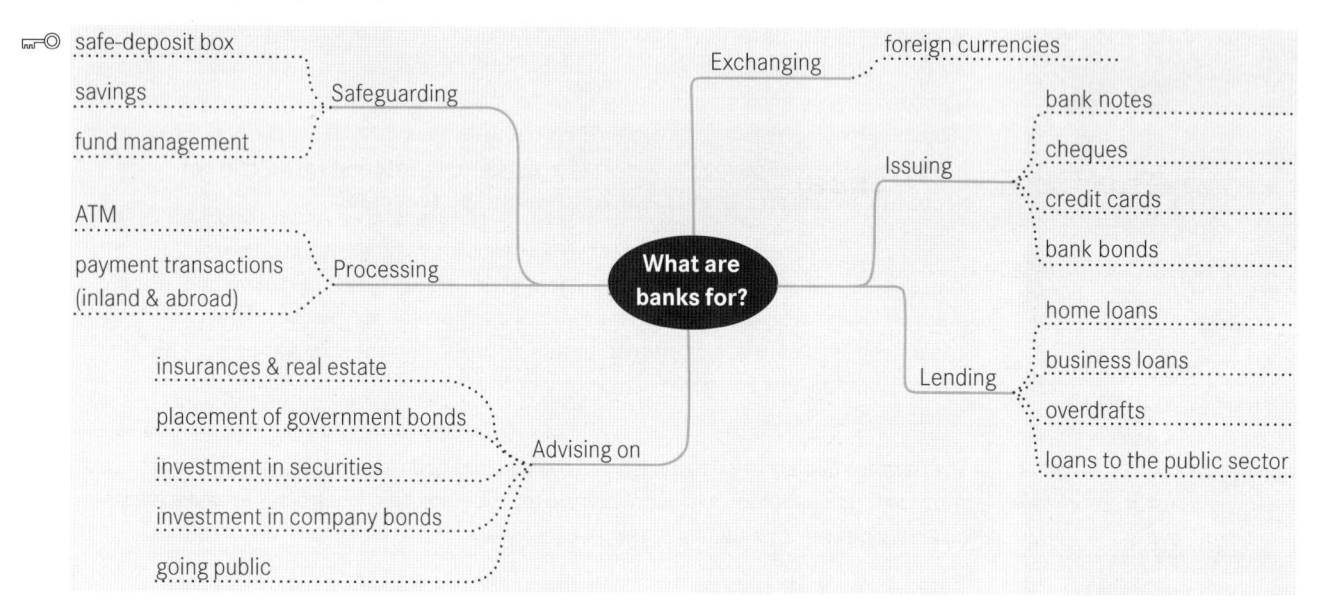

**What are banks for?**

- Safeguarding
  - safe-deposit box
  - savings
  - fund management
- Processing
  - ATM
  - payment transactions (inland & abroad)
- Advising on
  - insurances & real estate
  - placement of government bonds
  - investment in securities
  - investment in company bonds
  - going public
- Exchanging
  - foreign currencies
- Issuing
  - bank notes
  - cheques
  - credit cards
  - bank bonds
- Lending
  - home loans
  - business loans
  - overdrafts
  - loans to the public sector

**2** Form your students into pairs to complete this exercise. Remind them that they should invest in a comprehensive dictionary of English collocations to assist them research and learn word partnerships. They might also refer to online resources such as the following to establish which words can be partnered up to form strong collocations, http://www.americancorpus.org/

Point out that, while some of the verbs can be matched with different nouns, this exercise requires that each noun be matched with just one of the verbs so that eight "strong" collocations are formed. After allowing the pairs up to two minutes to work on the matches, bring the class back together to check answers and write the correct collocations on the board.

You may consider varying this routine – and injecting a spot of fun into your class – by completing the exercise using a kind of TV quiz format. If you choose to do this, small groups of three or four students should compete against each other to find each match in turn. Correct answers get one point: if a team answers incorrectly, the other teams get a chance to attempt another answer. You should play the role of quiz master, injecting humor into the occasion by using a "TV voice": however, the fun over, be sure to confirm what the correct answers are by writing them on the board.

Should you be pressed for time in class, you might also set this exercise as homework, checking and confirming the answers at the next lesson.

- be entitled to a grant
- charge a penalty fee
- control one's spending
- cover living expenses
- draw up a budget plan
- exceed one's overdraft limit
- grant an overdraft facility
- open a current account

**3** Tell the students that this exercise will offer them an opportunity to confirm the exact definitions of the word partnerships they have identified in exercise 2. They should work on their own to complete the sentences with the collocations. Should you wish to save on class time, consider setting this in tandem with exercise 2 as homework. When checking answers you might choose to spend a few minutes eliciting other collocations which feature some of the words here that the students may know of: *be entitled to a pension; stay within one's overdraft limit, go overdrawn on a current account,* etc.

62

# Debts, savings and investments 8

1 For making or receiving regular payments you need to <u>open a current account</u>.
2 If you <u>draw up a budget plan</u> you know precisely how much money you need during a month. This will stop you from <u>exceeding the overdraft limit</u> which your bank has offered you.
3 If you take out more money than there is in your bank account without prior agreement, the bank will <u>charge a penalty fee</u>.
4 Some universities offer special grants for students. Check out the details to find out if you <u>are entitled to a grant</u>.

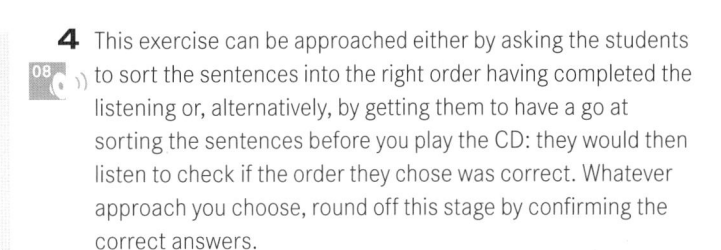

**4** This exercise can be approached either by asking the students to sort the sentences into the right order having completed the listening or, alternatively, by getting them to have a go at sorting the sentences before you play the CD: they would then listen to check if the order they chose was correct. Whatever approach you choose, round off this stage by confirming the correct answers.

1 e, 2 f, 3 b, 4 i, 5 d, 6 a, 7 g, 8 j, 9 h, 10 c
The Student Union advises students to draw up a budget plan.

## Discussion: **The banks' interest**

Form your students into groups for the ensuing discussion which you should give them up to ten minutes to complete. Encourage your students in their comparisons with their British counterparts by prompting with slightly provocative questions: *So, do you think British students have a tougher time of it than you do?* Similarly, provoke students into considering the banker's perspective with statements such as *Well, a bank's a business, isn't it? It's not the bank's fault if customers can't use its services responsibly.* Ask them to use the collocations from exercise 2 in the course of their discussions:

before the discussion begins, each student should write the collocations on a sheet of paper and cross them out one by one as they use them.

Then bring the class back together, getting volunteers to summarize the results of the discussion: encourage a full discussion across the class by inviting other students to interject their own observations or stating the ways in which they disagree and stating the grounds they have for this. Your students should remain in their groups for the next exercise.

## Diversity: **Savings habits across cultures**

Begin by asking your students to read over the *Diversity* box quickly with the aim of being able to summarize its contents. The skim reading over, ask two or three students to summarize what the text says. After the first student has described the first part of the box ask the next student to pick up where their classmate left off and so on.

You may choose to refocus the nature of the groups' discussion by asking students to consider not only the extent to which the various factors affect savings habits, but also the ways in which they influence them. Tell the students that you will pause for their feedback about this before they move on to consider which other factors may be at play: allow them around ten minutes for the first phase of their discussion before bringing the class back together.

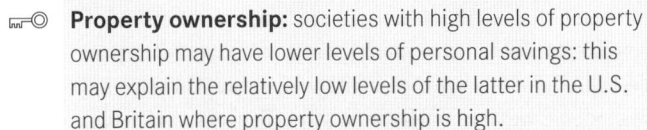

**Property ownership:** societies with high levels of property ownership may have lower levels of personal savings: this may explain the relatively low levels of the latter in the U.S. and Britain where property ownership is high.
**A positive or negative economic climate:** a negative economic climate may encourage people to hold onto what cash they have so that they can provide for themselves in the event of unemployment or the like.

**A positive attitude towards the future:** some cultures – for instance, that of the U.S. – tend to take a more sanguine view of the future which may lead to people saving less money for use "on a rainy day".
**The availability of a public safety net:** a highly-developed public safety net may encourage people to spend rather than save as they know that they will be provided for should their economic fortunes change. However, this may not always be the case as the lack of public safety net in the U.S. apparently doesn't lead to higher levels of savings while Germany's generous welfare system doesn't seem to dissuade many Germans from salting their cash away.
**Free education:** a free education system may encourage people to spend rather than save their money so that they can see to their children's education.
**A developed consumer credit system:** this may encourage or discourage savings – on the one hand people may save more and consume on credit; on the other, they may spend what money they could have saved servicing their credit card repayments.

Now ask your students to consider the final questions before bringing the class back together.

63

# 8 Debts, savings and investments

🔑 **Other possible factors:**
- interest rates
- the extent to which consumer culture has been developed in a society
- average rates of earnings
- the extent to which a "shareholder" culture has been developed in a society, i.e. while North Americans don't tend to save much, many ordinary Americans invest money they might otherwise have saved in shares and other investment vehicles

🔑 The apparently relaxed attitude of British and North American students to debt may be explained by attitudes to saving and a generally sanguine view of the future. However, it should be noted that, while British students now amass personal debt with as much gusto as their North American counterparts, this might cause rather more anxiety among British students. In the U.S. the notion that you "pay your way through college" (and this, to some extent, by drawing on lines of personal credit) has been established for generations. In the U.K., on the other hand, the current system of student finance is more recent: it may well be the case that British students amass debt rather less willingly.

## Reading: Types of investment

**1** The next two exercises will provide your students with an abundance of vocabulary used to talk about investments and investing. As it is likely that much of the vocabulary will be unknown to students, it will almost certainly be worth allowing them to complete the exercise with access to dictionaries. Have plenty of English dictionaries on hand. In any case, it will be worth allowing students to complete the table in exercise 1 in pairs, as decisions about which columns to place the expressions in are bound to provoke collaborative discussion.

Alternatively, you may choose to assign the completion of the table as homework to save time in the classroom.

| Types of assets | Investment criteria | Costs of asset management |
|---|---|---|
| property | yield | initial charge |
| issue | gain | safe custody charge |
| securities | liquid/liquidity | commission |
| currency futures | return | management fee |
| money-market | credit rating | waive |
| funds | performance | |
| equity | dividend | |
| | maturity | |
| | discount | |
| | denomination | |
| | credit risk | |

**2** If your students completed exercise 1 as homework, have them do this exercise at home as well. Remind them that they will have to manipulate the form of some of the expressions.

| | | | | | |
|---|---|---|---|---|---|
| 1 | yield | 4 | liquid | 7 | performance |
| 2 | issued | 5 | waive | 8 | equity |
| 3 | returns | 6 | gains | | |

**3** Warm your students up for the reading by asking them what types of investments they have heard of or may have made themselves. Stimulate their thinking with a few questions: *How would you finance a car?; How did your parents finance their home? How would a company finance a new building?*

Collect their suggestions on the board. Now ask if any of them, or anyone they know, has invested in any of the investment vehicles they have mentioned. Can they say why these particular types of investment were chosen?

Now pair off your students and ask them to read the instructions. Point out to the students that, while they will have to read the texts fairly closely, they may encounter some vocabulary which they don't know: they should attempt to arrive at the meaning of this by examining the context it appears in. Remind your students that they should try to think of words they know which are similar to any expressions they are not immediately familiar with *(volatile – volatility, substantially – substantial)* in order to guess intelligently the meaning of unknown terms. Tell your students that you will explain any particularly problematic vocabulary at the end of the exercise.

Your students should now read the texts on their own before carrying out the matching and listing of the strengths and weaknesses of one of the types of investors with their partners. Be sure that each type of investment is being covered by at least one pair of students for the purposes of the latter task.

You may consider a different approach for the matching phase of the task. While one student in a pair reads about the investment type, the other reads about the types of investors. Then, through description of what they have individually read, the students can attempt the matching. This approach, while upping the communicative ante of the exercise, should only be attempted with the most competent of readers.

# Debts, savings and investments  8

Encourage the pairs to report the pros and cons in the form of a mini-presentation with an introduction, main argument and conclusion. Allow up to 20 minutes for the reading and pair work discussions before bringing the class back together to collect answers. Round off by confirming the meaning of unknown vocabulary including *substantial*, *novice*, *volatility* and *conventional wisdom*. Point out that the phrasebook contains comprehensive coverage of the vocabulary from the texts.

|  | **Strengths** | **Weaknesses** | **Type of investor** |
|---|---|---|---|
| **Shares** | • shares mean ownership; therefore investors have a claim on the assets and earnings of a company (voting rights and dividend)<br>• shares mean equity, bonds are debt<br>• investors can make a lot of money<br>• shares are highly liquid (can be sold and bought easily) | • investors could lose all of their investment | **B** The moderate investor:<br>• investors who want to create wealth<br>• investors who know that this type of investment involves a certain risk |
| **Bonds** | • aren't infected by the volatility of the stock market (low risk) | • performance is lower than shares | **A** The conservative investor:<br>• investor who want a regular income after retirement<br>• if money is needed for a specific purpose in the relatively near future |
| **Futures** | • very risky and complex; the risk can slightly be reduced by using a good broker | • investors need a solid understanding of how the market and contracts function; they also need to determine how much time, attention, and research they can dedicate to the investment | **C** The adventurous investor:<br>• investors who are prepared to take a risk as the futures market is highly volatile – it is impossible to predict long- or short-term performance |
| **Commercial paper (CP)** | • safe investment because the financial situation of a company can be easily predicted over a few months<br>• credit ratings are available<br>• offer lower returns than riskier investments | • suitable only for big investors<br>• can be turned into cash quickly (liquid) | **C** The adventurous investor:<br>• small investors get access to CP through market money funds |
| **Unit trusts** | • diversification of investors' investment<br>• monthly contributions are possible<br>• the fund is managed by a professional fund manager (convenience) | • performance of unit trusts are in general below market average<br>• commission fee can be quite high<br>• the management fee has to be paid whether the fund actually makes gains or not | **D** The contrarian investor:<br>• investors with small funds which are not large enough to achieve a reasonable degree of diversification<br>• investors who don't want to be bothered with the management of their funds |

### Business Skills

## Negotiating: **Achieving a good deal**

**1** Ask your students to read the instructions and the statements in the speech bubbles, then ask which statements the students agree with and why. As several of the statements are matters of opinion, encourage further discussion by inviting students to disagree with one another. Round off this stage by getting the class to summarize the gist of their discussion in a few guidelines about negotiating.

Write this on the board along the following lines.
- Prepare for a negotiation by doing your homework.
- Have several outcomes which are acceptable to you up your sleeve.
- Listen carefully to what your negotiating partner has to say.

# 8 Debts, savings and investments

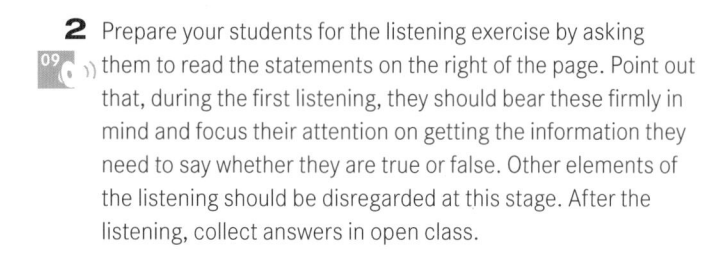

**2** Prepare your students for the listening exercise by asking them to read the statements on the right of the page. Point out that, during the first listening, they should bear these firmly in mind and focus their attention on getting the information they need to say whether they are true or false. Other elements of the listening should be disregarded at this stage. After the listening, collect answers in open class.

🔑 1 **true**, 2 **false**, 3 **false**, 4 **true**, 5 **false**, 6 **true**

**3** Before playing the CD again, you may choose to ask your students to recount what they recollect about the agreement reached. Ask them to bear these recollections in mind as they listen again in order to check their accuracy. In any case, the students should be in a position to summarize the agreement between Deborah and her financial advisor after the second listening.

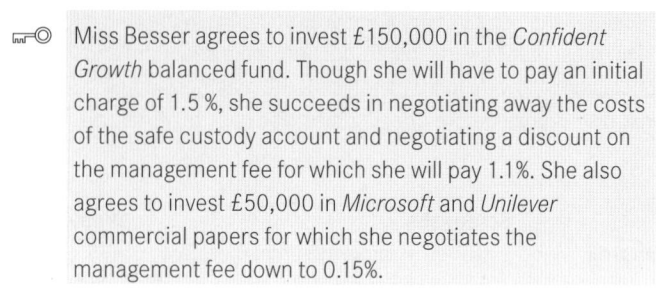

🔑 Miss Besser agrees to invest £150,000 in the *Confident Growth* balanced fund. Though she will have to pay an initial charge of 1.5 %, she succeeds in negotiating away the costs of the safe custody account and negotiating a discount on the management fee for which she will pay 1.1%. She also agrees to invest £50,000 in *Microsoft* and *Unilever* commercial papers for which she negotiates the management fee down to 0.15%.

**4** Put your students into small groups to consider the remaining questions. Extend the first question by asking the students to consider additionally how they as individuals would have invested the cash. Allow up to ten minutes for the groups to discuss the questions before bringing the class back together and to discuss the results of the students' deliberations.

## Negotiating: The key stages

**1** Ask your students to close their books and play the CD track again. Before doing so, set the class the task of listening in order to decide what the distinct phases which make up a negotiation are. The listening over, ask for suggestions as to what the phases are writing these on the board. Don't concern yourself with the terminology the students use to describe these at this stage.

In all probability your students will come up with something which resembles the model described in the Course Book. Congratulate the class and ask them to open their books at page 79.

Split the students into pairs giving them a minute to look over the mind map, then ask a couple of students to describe the phases of a negotiation represented by it. Press for further information by asking questions like *What sort of things would people tend to say at this stage* and *Which phrases might you expect to hear at this point in a negotiation?* Finally, ask a student to summarize briefly what the task is and ensure that everyone knows the meaning of *firm*. Give the students five minutes to complete the mind map.

**2** Now allow your students to check and add to their answers by playing the CD track once more. In order to avoid misunderstandings, however, it will be worth quickly going over the answers with the class.

### Negotiating the best deal

Split your students into pairs or small groups giving each pair or group a well-shuffled set of cut up strips. Tell the students that the utterances make up a dialog similar to the preceding listening: the dialog here, however, features phrases for negotiating which, though close in meaning to those used in the listening, are worded somewhat differently. Their task now comes in two parts. First they should reassemble the dialog putting the utterances in logical order. They should then turn to the audioscript of the listening on pages 151–152 of the Course Book and match the synonymous phrases from the photocopiable activity and the listening.

Allow your students some five minutes to complete the first stage before bringing the class back together to check answers. Next allow a further few minutes for the students to match the phrases. Again confirm the correct phrase matches with the class.

# Debts, savings and investments    8

| Negotiation stage | Purpose | Phrase |
|---|---|---|
| Discussing | Checking what the other party wants | What do you want to invest for?<br>Would you like to use the whole amount for …?<br>What are the conditions?<br>What do you have in mind? |
| Proposing | Making suggestions | What I would recommend is investing in …<br>Let me suggest …<br>What about …?<br>I could offer you … |
| Bargaining | Firm | (As far as the management fee is concerned) I can't go below 1.25%.<br>(OK, but) I can only guarantee you this for three years.<br>I think you should be offering me better conditions. |
| | Compromising | I think I could make an exception (and waive the trading account charges.)<br>I see your point, (so) I could reduce the commission for… |
| | Confrontational | Alright, but only under the condition that (I get the safe custody account for free.)<br>I'm sorry but that's not good enough. |
| Reaching an agreement | Summarizing | I think we have a deal.<br>Let me summarize what we have agreed upon … |

## Negotiating: **Getting what you need**

Split your students into new pairs telling each who will be *A* and *B*. Allow the students time to read the instructions, situation and their own roles the contents of which they should not disclose to their partners. Point out that they need to do as much fact finding about their partners' needs as possible in order to complete the negotiation with a win-win solution. Remind them of the language for negotiating which they encountered on page 79 and refer them to the *Useful expressions* list on page 167: they should each select at least four phrases from the lists which they should aim to use in the course of their negotiation.

Now set the students loose on their task listening in on as many negotiations as possible. As you do so, take note of any mistakes or clumsy formulations which you would like to feed back to the class for self correction later. At the same time, don't forget to note things the students do particularly well and congratulate them on these later.

When the negotiations are complete, get each pair to state briefly the outcome of their negotiation. Clearly, the most obvious win-win outcome would be that they peel the orange and each student take the part of it they are most interested in. However, should other solutions be mentioned, be sure to ask the students which solution is most sensible in the end. Finally, write any mistakes or clumsy formulations you want the students to address on the board asking for suggestions for improvement.

## Role-play: **Negotiate your dream car**

Ask your students to close their books and split them into new pairs, assigning them their roles. *Student As* should now open their books at page 126 and *Student Bs* at page 80. The students should take a few minutes to read the situation and study their roles as well as the phrases in their respective language boxes. They should select four phrases from the latter which they should aim to use during the role-play. Remind them also of the phrases they selected from page 79 and page 167 for use in the negotiating exercise at the top of page 80 and encourage them to attempt to use these phrases again as well.

Now bring all the *As* together at one end of the classroom and the *Bs* at the other giving the students five minutes to discuss their roles and the terms they would personally be prepared to come to in the negotiation. When you feel that the students have prepared themselves adequately, re-form the role-play pairs and give the students up to 15 minutes to carry out the role-play.

Listen in during the role-plays noting, on this occasion, successful and appropriate use of phrases from the language boxes: take a note of these so that you can congratulate students later. When the role-plays are over, get each pair to describe in some detail what terms they agreed on. Once the class has been told the results of each negotiating, ask the students to discuss which bank advisor struck the best deal from the bank's perspective and which student secured the best terms for the loan. Finally, draw attention to the phrases you noted earlier and congratulate all your students on the successful completion of the role-play.

# 8 Debts, savings and investments

## Company Case: Finding the right partner overseas

Before splitting your students into groups, warm them up for the reading by asking what they understand by the term *ethical banking*. Be sure to draw attention to which of their suggestions are accurate and in line with the concept.

The students should now study the questions and work in their groups. Make it clear that they should structure their reports clearly and that several students should be involved in delivering the report, each of the sections mentioned could be assigned to a student for reporting back. You should consider allowing the groups up to 25 minutes for reading, discussion and the structuring of reports.

Invite each group to deliver their reports allowing a couple of minutes at the end of each turn during which other students can "cross-examine" the report's authors.

1. So far *GBI Bank* has only gained business experience in the European market. The Brazilian market seems to be less regulated and requires different business approaches. It has a different cultural environment, so problems could occur if and when European managers suddenly initiate changes.

2. *Acosta Real's* reputation has suffered so much that a new beginning is necessary: a new name, a new image and a new management could help.
The effect of a turn-around will not be felt immediately with the consequence that the bank will continue losing customers.
But with *GBI*'s know-how and good reputation there is a fair chance of a turn-around.

3. The investment in *Acosta Real* won't produce any return at the beginning, just the opposite: *GBI* will have additional costs because know-how also has its price. However, having a stake in the Brazilian bank would meet *GBI*'s ethical goals. So Acosta Real's offer is worth considering.

## Over to you

### Web research: Finding the right bank

Encourage your students to complete this exercise. You might want to extend the scope of the exercise by setting the students the task of identifying the market-leading banks in the countries they are looking at.

Ask the students to appoint a "research co-ordinator". They should send the results of their research to this student in advance of the next class: s/he should consolidate the data in a table so that students can examine it. In the next class you could use the table as a springboard for discussion about the contrast in conditions offered by banks in the countries covered.

### Reading: Islamic finance makes a move into the mainstream

Find out more about Islamic banking by visiting the following websites:

http://www.islamic-bank.com/
http://www.islamic-banking.com/

**1**

| Conventional banks | Islamic banks |
| --- | --- |
| • pay interest on savings and current accounts | • do not pay interest on current accounts |
| • charge interest on overdrafts, loans and mortgages | • grant investors partial ownership on real assets |
| • pay interest to investors | • share profits with holders of saving accounts |

**2**
- Home owners with a mortgage from an Islamic bank are protected from the volatility of the financial markets by having to pay back a fixed amount which was agreed upon at the beginning of the transaction.
- Sharia-compliant bonds are asset-based: instead of receiving interest, bond holders receive "rent" on the asset. This means that investors are protected against those bond providers who use borrowed money to boost their profits on their investment.

**3** 1 b, 2 f, 3 a, 4 e, 5 d, 6 c

**4** Encourage students to use a clear structure when writing their paragraphs which should comprise an introductory sentence explaining what the text is about, the main body of argument and a conclusion. Invite students to email their writing to you so that you can comment upon it.

# 9 Company structure

## Self Study

**Vocabulary**
- The departments of a company
- Positions in company hierarchy
- Using reporting verbs: alternatives to *say* and *tell*

**Grammar**
- Get the verb right: *say* or *tell*?
- Reported speech: what the boss said
- Comparing and contrasting: types of organizations

**Skills**
- Opening and closing a meeting
- Meetings: confirming attendance and apologizing for absence
- Meetings: what's in the minutes?

**Reading**
- The human cost of corporate reorganization: reading closely
- In other words

**Video**
- Preparing for a meeting
- Heard in the meeting: typical phrases
- Meeting phrases and what they do for you
- Meeting phrases: know how to use them
- Three years on

## At a glance

The topic of this unit – how companies choose to structure themselves – is a subject which constantly occupies senior managers irrespective of what business they work in. Of course, many companies persist in structuring themselves in a centralized and hierarchical fashion. However, since the 1980s businesses have invested much time and money in examining how they can decentralize their organizational structures. The unit explores the rationale behind these restructuring efforts and enables students to reflect on the bigger picture.

Completion of the unit will put students in the position to discuss the organizational challenges confronting businesses. As well as examining the characteristics of **decentralization** and **centralization** in company organization – **ambiguity**, **distributed power** and **open structure** versus **coercive power**, **norms** and **command** – students will look at the functional distinctions between horizontal and vertical types of organization.

The focus of the *Business Skills* section of the unit – meetings – dovetails neatly with its central theme. Meetings are, after all, a key means of communication within a company irrespective of its structure. However, the character of meetings within a business will be largely determined by the organizational model it has chosen for itself.

As well as providing a short historical overview of developments in organizational theory, this readable article provides a summary of contemporary approaches to organization in business:
http://www.enotes.com/small-business-encyclopedia/organization-theory

For a fuller discussion of the rationales behind business organization *The Starfish and the Spider: The Unstoppable Power of Leaderless Organizations* is an interesting read.

## Warm-up

Divide your students into small groups and ask them to discuss the differing organizational styles of the leaders featured in the Course Book. It may be the case that they will need further information regarding some of the examples. Prompt their thinking with questions, such as *Anita Roddick was the founder of The Body Shop which is well-known for promoting employee involvement. What sort of leadership style do you think she had?* or *Mahatma Gandhi led a mass movement of peaceful protest. What might his approach to leadership have been?*

Allow five minutes for discussion before bringing the class back together and collecting feedback. Treat this as an opportunity to assist your students with some basic formulation of key expressions about leadership which they will need as the unit progresses. Your students should remain in their groups for the next exercise.

# 9 Company structure

## Listening: Spider and starfish organizations

**1** Draw the students' attention to the table, allowing the groups up to ten minutes to discuss the characteristics typical of centralized and decentralized organizations. Encourage students to work collaboratively within their groups to arrive at the meaning of unknown vocabulary. Be prepared to provide definitions of unknown terms should students not be able to do so themselves. Explain *ambiguity, coercive power, command* and *distributed power*.

Invite students to share their own experiences of any companies they may have worked in and say whether they were centralized or decentralized in nature. Encourage them to use any new vocabulary that they have just encountered.

|  | centralization | decentralization | both | neither |
|---|---|---|---|---|
| ambiguity |  | ✓ |  |  |
| anarchy |  |  |  | ✓ |
| CEO | ✓ |  |  |  |
| coercive power | ✓ |  |  |  |
| command | ✓ |  |  |  |
| control | ✓ |  |  |  |
| distributed power |  | ✓ |  |  |
| flexibility |  | ✓ |  |  |
| headquarters | ✓ |  |  |  |
| hierarchy | ✓ |  |  |  |
| leader |  |  | ✓ |  |
| leadership by example |  | ✓ |  |  |
| norms |  |  | ✓ |  |
| open structure |  | ✓ |  |  |
| rules |  |  | ✓ |  |
| shared power |  | ✓ |  |  |

**2** Tell your students that they are now going to listen to an excerpt from a book discussing centralized and decentralized organizational structures. Allow them time to read the preamble to the listening, then explain that their task during the first run-through of the listening is to check their answers to exercise 1 on page 84. Now ask your students if there was anything they found surprising about the way Apaches organized themselves. Play the track again and ask students to note what is said about Apache organization and what Nevins says about centralized and decentralized organizations. After this second listening ask for volunteers to provide an overview of Apache organization. One student could summarize what Nevins says about centralized organizations and another could summarize his argument regarding decentralized organizations.

**3** Ask the class if anyone knows what *NGO* stands for and whether they can offer any examples of NGOs.

Now pair off your students so they can discuss the virtues of centralization and decentralization for each type of organization. When the time is up, bring the class back together and ask the pairs to summarize their conclusions. Allow a few more minutes for discussion during which the students should debate any discrepancies between the conclusions they reached.

1 **Universities** display characteristics of both centralized and decentralized approaches to organization. On the one hand, they tend to display centralized characteristics under the leadership of chairs. On the other, individual academics usually have a free hand as to which research they carry out.
2 **NGOs** often have an international headquarters and international leadership but strongly decentralized local chapters. Decentralization at the local level allows staff and volunteers to respond appropriately to local circumstances.
3 **Many self-help organizations** are highly decentralized. The reasoning behind this is that the groups exist for their members and that it is they who should decide on the direction of their activities.
4 **Car manufacturers** tend to be highly centralized, they are large organizations which need central direction to meet the high degree of standardization required by production in the industry.
5 **Armies** tend to be highly centralized. The purpose of this centralization is to create clear and effective lines of command which is crucial to success in conflict situations.

**Company structure** 9

## Reading: The structure of organizations

**1** Ask your students to turn their attention to the three questions. Allow them five minutes to consider their answers before encouraging a whole-class discussion.

**2** Your students should now turn their attention to the reading exercise. Ensure that they understand that their task is to read the text to find the answers to the three questions. They should disregard unknown vocabulary or other elements of the text they don't understand in the meantime. After reading, they should work with their partners to answer the questions.

Confirm the correct answers in open class.

> 1 The structure of an organization is determined by two important factors. The first are external considerations such as the demands imposed by markets and the political environment. The level of complexity involved in the task is the second crucial factor.
> 2 A company might change its structure in response to shifts in the business environment, to keep the people leading the company in touch with realities on the shop floor or to allow employees to feel that they have a stake in decision-making processes.
> 3 The author predicts that, owing to the development of communications technology, large, previously centralized organizations will introduce elements of decentralization into their structures. He also predicts a growth in P2P (peer to peer) networking.

**3** Your students should continue working in their pairs to complete this matching exercise. It may be the case that some students already know the vocabulary items – or have gathered their meaning from their reading of the text: they should be able to complete the matching relatively swiftly. Ask students who are less sure of what some words mean to examine how they are used in the text and encourage them to arrive at the definitions through considering the context. Confirm the correct answers in open class and prompt your students to copy the words into their notebooks.

> 1 e, 2 a, 3 g, 4 b, 5 c, 6 f, 7 d

Invite your students to explore the text further and underline words or expressions they don't understand. Expect them to raise questions about the words *accomplish*, *differentiation* and *cut and dried*. Avoid the temptation to define these yourself and remind them that the meaning of unknown vocabulary can often be arrived at through considering the context that it is used in. Invite the students to do just this allowing the pairs several minutes for their research. Collect their attempted definitions in open class.

**4** Your students' final task is to use the language from the text to describe the four diagrams. Should you think that your students will find this difficult, you may want to model the exercise using one of the diagrams with the whole class. To do this, start the ball rolling yourself by posing one or two questions: *So does this look like a centralized or decentralized organization?* Invite answers from the class prompting students who contribute to go on with their description. Your students should now complete descriptions of the remaining diagrams: Allow no more than five minutes for this.

Bring the class back together to collect answers and congratulate your students on their appropriate use of the target language.

Extend the exercise further by introducing a final step. Ask the pairs to think about which diagrams the companies mentioned in the text could probably be matched up with. As the students don't have much information about the companies and have to make educated assumptions, you will have to leave some room for error here. However, asking your students to complete this stage will stimulate further discussion using the target language, so when you bring the class back together to compare answers, allow time for this discussion.

> A tall, highly centralized organizational structure with 7 tiers
> B partially decentralized organizational structure
> C flat structure with only two tiers
> D highly decentralized organization (possibly P2P)

## Diversity: Organization and culture

Preamble this section by asking your students if they feel that the way companies are organized is influenced by the national cultures the companies come from. Should some students have definite ideas one way or the other, ask them if they can provide a few examples to justify their thinking.

Now ask your students to close their books while you write *incubator*, *guided missile*, *Eiffel Tower* and *family* on the board. You might also want to supply some pictures of the terms to allow students to spark their creativity and explain the meaning of *incubator* and *guided missile*. Tell them that these are metaphors which have been applied to different types of company culture and encourage students to say what sort of culture and organization within a company each term might describe. Write their suggestions on the board without commenting upon them.

71

# 9 Company structure

Now ask your students to open their books and examine the diagram to see if any of their suggestions proved accurate. Round this stage up with the whole class by prompting students to describe each type of company culture in their own words.

If students' suggestions proved accurate, emphasize this and congratulate them.

Your students should now turn their attention to answering the questions. Allow around five minutes for them to do so, then round off the activity by discussing their answers.

## Discussion: **Talking about organigrams**

**1** Copy the organigram onto a transparent slide and project it onto the wall using an overhead projector. Write the vocabulary items from the box on the board.

Now familiarize your students with the target vocabulary by asking them questions using the key lexis, such as: *Which three directors are accountable to Tim Howard?* or *Who does Tim Howard report to?*

Where possible reiterate target vocabulary focussing on different interdepartmental relationships from the organigram. Ideally, the pace of this question and answer phase should be quite rapid: increase the speed of your questioning further as you sense that students are getting the hang of the target lexis.

Your students should now complete the gaps in the text with the appropriate vocabulary. Confirm the correct answer.

> 1 division;  2 units;  3 reported to;  4 responsible for;
> 5 subordinates;  6 accountable to

**2** Put your students into small groups to work on this exercise. Make sure that they understand their task by quickly asking one or two students to reiterate the instructions in their own words. Help students who have no work experience to come up with ideas: you might prompt their thinking by asking if they are members of a sports club or a project group at university. Make sure that each student has an organization to talk about before asking everybody to describe their experiences within their groups. Tell the students that they are to take mental note of what other group members say. To ensure that this stage doesn't take too long, set a time limit of about three minutes for each student. Tell the students that they should quickly draw their organigram when the discussion is over.

You can turn the students' descriptions of their organizations into material for whole-class work in the following way. Ask one or two students from each group to report what others in the group described putting them in the position of having to actively recall other students' descriptions and to use reported speech: *Karen said she works part-time in a supermarket where the structure is very hierarchical.*

### Organigram puzzle

Tell your students that they are going to reconstruct the organigram of the company behind a social networking website called *OurPlace*. Ask the class to brainstorm job titles that are likely to come up on an organigram of a company like this. Write their suggestions on the board.

Now pair up your students giving each pair a copy of the organigram and 13 of the 15 cards. Be sure that two different cards are missing from the card sets received by each pair. The students' first job is to reconstruct the organigram as far as possible by reading their cards. Set your students a time limit of ten minutes to complete the organigram with all the information from their 13 cards.

When they have finished, tell your students that all of their organigrams are incomplete but that they can fill two of the gaps by asking other pairs questions. Model the activity by saying *So, Niall Mitchell's the Finance Manager, right? But I don't have a name for the Finance Assistant.* Now point to a student and ask *Can you tell me who reports to Niall Mitchell, please?* None of the students will be able to answer this. What's the point of this? Emphasize that the students' task now is to circulate, putting similar questions featuring the target phrases for describing working relationships to other students until they collect two of the names missing from their organigram.

As the students mingle, listen in on their exchanges and note any mistakes you want to highlight for self-correction at the end of the activity. The mingling phase over, ask for volunteers to call out the names which they have attached to the job titles on the organigram. Confirm the correct answers and write the mistakes you noted earlier on the board. Encourage the class to correct them.

**Company structure** 9

**Business Skills**

## Meetings: **Getting ready**

**1** Animate this exercise further in the following way. After your students have spent a minute reading and reflecting on the attitudes about meetings, ask them to decide which statements they agree with most. Now focus on each statement in turn and ask volunteers to say briefly why they agree or disagree giving quick examples from their own experience if possible. Prompt students to elaborate on their experiences by posing pertinent questions. For instance, students who feel that meetings are boring could be encouraged to say more through questions such as *What was the most boring meeting you ever went to?* Similarly, students who feel that meetings are an opportunity for getting to know others might be asked *Did you ever find out something about a person in a meeting that you didn't know before?*

The previous stage will have given you a notion as to which students regard meetings positively and which regard them negatively. Now split the class into two groups: the first will draw up a list of the advantages to an organization of meetings; the second will list the disadvantages. Try to put as many students as possible who take a dim view of meetings in the "advantages" group and vice versa: however, be pragmatic about this to keep the groups roughly of equal size. Give the students five minutes for their deliberations before bringing the class back together. A volunteer from each group should summarize the list their group came up with: write these lists on the board assisting with formulation and feeding in any expressions which you think are begged by the points being made. Ensure that the students understand these and allow them a few minutes to write them into their notebooks.

**2** Begin by ensuring that your students understand the vocabulary and ask them the following questions. Which of these meetings is held:
- to report on the development of a product or project?
- to mark the beginning of a project?
- each year to report on an organization's progress?

*Team meeting* will be self-explanatory. Having established the meaning of the vocabulary, draw the following spider diagram on the board and invite students to call out any other types of meetings they may have heard of. Complete the diagram with their suggestions assisting with correct formulation where necessary.

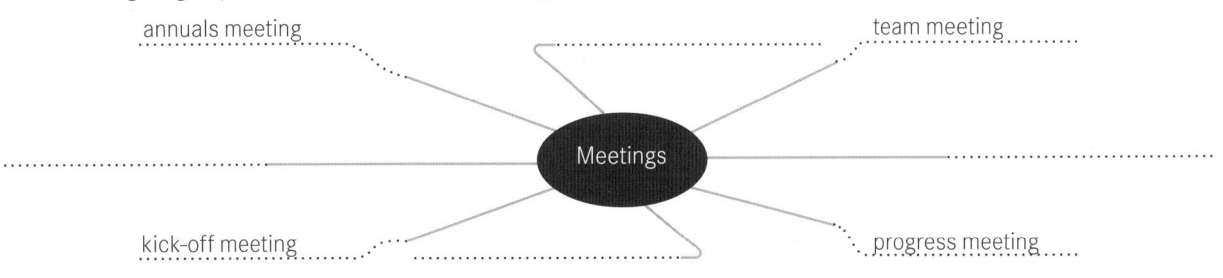

annuals meeting     team meeting

Meetings

kick-off meeting     progress meeting

🔑 Students may mention *brainstorming meeting, sales meeting, interdepartmental meeting, appraisal meeting, shareholder meeting* and/or *board meeting*.

Turn your students attention to the emails asking them to read these as swiftly as they can in order to gain a sense of the type of meeting they refer to. Collect their answers in open class.

🔑 A kick-off meeting
B progress meeting
C team meeting
D annual meeting

Now turn your students' attention back to the emails asking them to go over them again and consider which are formal, informal or somewhere in between in tone. They should look for evidence within the emails to justify their choices. Prompt individual students to call out their suggestions in open class and encourage a short discussion about the relative formality or informality of each of the emails.

🔑 A – Inspite of *Dear all*, email is relatively formal in tone
B – quite informal
C – very informal as evidenced by *Hi guys* and chatty tone
D – email is very formal in tone (*Dear shareholder, Sincerely yours*) = indistinguishable from a formal business letter

**3** Ensure that your students know the meaning of the word *agenda*. Encourage a brainstorming approach to the questions, and then collect answers in open class confirming which suggestions are correct and gently dismissing suggestions which miss the mark.

🔑 
- Emails A and D include an agenda.
- The purpose of an agenda is to inform participants of the objective of a meeting and to provide structure for the discussion so as to ensure effectiveness.
- The subject of a meeting, the location and date, starting and finishing times and occasionally the names of the participants expected to attend all belong in an agenda.
- An agenda might not be necessary for a very informal meeting with a small number of participants.

73

# 9 Company structure

## Meetings: Acting as the chair

**1** Explain to your class that in formal meetings a record is generally kept of what has been said and decided. Invite your students to scan the list of tasks in order to identify what this document is called: the *minutes*. Working in their groups the students should then discuss which tasks belong to the chairperson's remit. Confirm the correct answers

> It would generally not be a chairperson's role to take the minutes, explain decisions to participants or push through their own ideas.

**2** Ask your students to read over the agenda. Ask if anyone knows what *AOB* stands for: if no-one does, invite some suggestions and confirm the correct answer. Ask them to speculate about what this might be and confirm that it is the section of the meeting given over to matters not formally itemized on the agenda.

> This agenda also features the precise times that will be spent on each item as well as the times of breaks, AOB and the date and time of the next meeting.

**3**
**4** As these three listenings could be quite challenging for students, be sure to tackle each section in turn. Ask the
**5** students to read the questions, then listen for the answers. You can then collect answers before moving onto the next section where this procedure can be repeated.

> **3**
> - She welcomed the participants.
> - She apologized for an absent participant.
>
> **4**
> - The organizational structure of the company is to be changed. Whereas it used to function in regional divisions, it is to be reorganized into general business units by product category.
> - They begin speaking at the same time; some have become nervous or aggressive.
> - Margaret calls them to attention and sees to it that each gets a turn to speak.
>
> **5**
> - She sums up what has been discussed in an upbeat way and announces the approximate date of the next meeting.
> - Points in the agenda covered in the meeting: restructuring measures, date of next meeting and adjournment.

If you would like to pay particular attention to some of the functional phrases used by the chairperson in the meeting refer to the *Over to you* section on page 92. Here students are asked to find the relevant meeting phrases in the audioscript and match them with the correct function.

### Video: An Internship abroad: Meeting

You might consider referring to the video at this point. Ask your students to brainstorm what they think makes a good chair, then set them the task of assessing how well Rebecca performs in her role as chair of the meeting. They should consider how well prepared she is, how much opportunity she affords other participants to contribute, how she deals with participants going "off topic" and how she goes about seeking solutions to problems. Play the video clip up until the point when Nan makes her assessment of how well Rebecca performs, then pause at this point. Invite the students to say what they think about Rebecca's performance. They should give examples from the video to back up their opinions. Now play the video from the point that Nan makes her appraisal of Rebecca: Nan's appraisal provides in summary an accurate picture of Rebecca's qualities as a chair.

Now focus on the functional language used in the clip. Explain to your students that you will play it again and that you want them to listen for phrases used by any of the participants which have a functional character and might be used in other meetings. When they hear such a phrase they should call out *stop*, then give them a few moments to note the phrase.

> - In the main, we're here to discuss …
> - But first I have to inform you all about …
> - I apologize for being late.
> - I think this issue should be the main focus of our meeting today.
> - I'm not sure I can agree with you there.
> - But everyone recalls, …
> - Excuse me for interrupting, but …
> - May I come in here?
> - I think we should stick to the point.
> - What about …?
> - I'm afraid I don't quite understand you. Are you saying that …
> - Let me put it another way: …
> - I agree with …
> - Would anyone like to add anything?
> - It seems that we all agree so before we move onto the next point on the agenda can I hand the meeting back over to …

## 9 Company structure

### Meeting phrases matching game

This matching exercise, which is comprised of key phrases employed in meetings, can be used either as a game of Snap or a memory card game. You should pair off your students to play both these games. If you choose to play Snap, photocopy two sets of cards for each pair. For Memory, one set of cards per pair will suffice.

Before playing either of these games your students will have to match the phrases. Give each pair a set of cards and a few minutes to complete the matching. When they have finished, confirm the correct answers in open class and clarify the meaning of any phrases or expressions the students are unsure of.

To play Snap, give each pair their other set of cards and ask the students to shuffle all the cards thoroughly. The cards should now be dealt so that each player has an equal hand of 20 cards. The game works as follows. Players, who should at no point look at the cards in their hand, take turns putting a card face up in the center of the table. If someone puts down a card with the same meaning as the previous card, the first player to say *snap* and put their hand over the pile of cards in the center of the table, wins these cards. The game then continues in the same way: the player with the most "snapped" cards wins.

To play Memory, after the pairs have completed the initial matching, ask them to shuffle their cards thoroughly and lay them randomly face down on the table. Players take turns turning over two cards. If the cards match synonymously, the player to have turned them over claims them and lays them to the side. If the cards don't match, they are turned back over and the next player takes their turn. As the game progresses, the players should build up a picture of where matching cards are on the table so that they can match and claim them on their next turn. The game continues until all the matches have been made: the player with the most matched cards at the end wins.

### Role-play: **Committee work at university**

Tell your students that they are going to role-play a university committee meeting and allow them some time to read the situation box.

Divide your class into groups of six students and draw their attention to the agenda and the language box. Ask the students to identify which of the phrases would exclusively be used by the chair of the meeting and confirm the correct answers.

> We're here today to discuss …
> The first item on the agenda is …
> We're running short of time …

To save time, tell the students which roles they are to play and allow them time to read their role cards. The students should now read their roles. When they have done this, direct them to form groups with classmates who are playing the same role. Tell the class that you are going to talk quickly to each group. While students are waiting for you to come to their group they should select three phrases from the box which they should aim to use during the meeting. Go to each group and ensure that the students understand the role they are to play by asking one of them to summarize it in their own words.

Then ask the students to go back to their role-play groups and tell them that they have a time limit of 20 minutes to carry out the exercise. Remind them that they should aim to use the three phrases that they have selected in the course of the meeting.

Listen in on the different groups as they role-play and take note of any mistakes or positive examples that you hear which you want to draw attention to at the end. When the role-play is over, write the mistakes you have selected on the board and invite the class to correct these.

Ensure that all your students have a chance to practice writing: they should each write the email, then send it to you. Tell them that you will send back your comments before the next lesson.

### Company Case: **A marriage of convenience**

Begin work on the case study by asking your students if they know what a *marriage of convenience* is. Drawing attention to the photo, prompt students to say whether such a partnership is likely to be a happy one. Ask the class to speculate about what the text might say in the light of this title and the photo, and note suggestions on the board. Now ask your students to read swiftly over the text to gain a general understanding of it and see if any of their speculations proved accurate.

75

# 9 Company structure

The students should then read and answer the questions. Rather than simply asking students to read out their answers, round off by encouraging a classroom discussion about the questions. Students can use their written answers as a springboard for the discussion.

1. Students may be aware of these stereotypes. Germans are seen as hyper-disciplined and efficient, sticklers for rules, and a people with an under-developed sense of humor.
   Common stereotypes of Americans include that they are poorly informed, politically and religiously conservative, and lacking culture and manners.
2. American employees would probably have trouble with the rigid chain of demand. German executives might not like reporting to more than one boss.
3. The emphasis on teamwork could be unusual for many Germans. Especially older German executives might dislike being addressed by their first names. They may also mistake the use of first names as familiarity which is not necessarily the case.

Encourage students to go into as much detail as possible designing their plans, including, for instance, proposed timeframes for individual elements of the plan or the content of any intercultural training they may want to include. Give each group a time limit of five minutes for their presentations.

## Over to you

### Meetings: Knowing what to say

1 Remind your students of the benefits to their writing of structuring their paragraph clearly. It should open with a sentence stating the drift of what will be argued, contain a clearly organized progression of the argument and conclude with a sentence which summarizes the argument.

2 **Calling the meeting to order:** *Can we get started?*
**Saying when the coffee break is:** *We'll be breaking for coffee around 11 o'clock.*
**Saying you'll start with the second point on the agenda:** *Unfortunately, we'll have to skip the first item ...*
**Saying (...) has permission to speak:** *Could we give you the floor?*
**Calling the participants to order:** *Sorry, could I have your attention please?*
**Referring to the handout:** *If you look at the handout, you can see that ...*
**Asking participants to speak one after the other:** *Let's take it in turns.*
**Saying how much you have accomplished:** *Well, I think we've covered quite a lot of territory for today.*
**Summing up the discussion:** *To recap briefly, ...*
**Finishing the meeting:** *I'd like to close the official part of our meeting.*

### Writing: Expressing a point of view

1 
| Sentence | Function |
| --- | --- |
| 1 | paraphrase of the author's position |
| 2 | statement of your position |
| 3 | your first supporting argument or example |
| 4 | a further supporting argument or example |
| 5 | your final supporting argument or example |
| 6 | a summary of your position |

# 10 Accounting

## Self Study

**Vocabulary**
- Who's who in accounting?
- Accounting collocations
- Finding words in the same family

**Grammar**
- Combining adjectives with adverbs
- Conditionals: how likely is it?
- Conditionals: speculation, speculation

**Skills**
- What you own and what you owe: balance sheet terminology
- Talking about balance sheets
- Softening your criticism

**Reading**
- Appreciating depreciation: Reading closely
- Dealing with unfamiliar words

## At a glance

Some of your students may not feel that accounting is the most fascinating subject on their university curriculum. This unit, however, will leave them in no doubt as to its importance in business and the far-reaching consequences of crooked accounting practices.

Through its examination of the *Enron* case, one of the largest cases of accounting fraud in the last several years, the unit will furnish students with fundamental accounting lexis such as **chief financial officer (CFO), creditor, debtor, auditor, goodwill, entity, certified public accountant (CPA)** and **net value** but also appropriate language for discussing cases of accounting malpractice including **whistle blowing, to massage the figures** and **fraud**.

The unit's *Business Skills* section continues the focus on lexis equipping students with the terminology for key financial statements such as **profit and loss account, balance sheet** and **cash flow statement**. However, rather than taking a dry approach, this section of the unit examines another large case of accounting fraud, that of *Satyam Computer Services*. Thus your students get the chance to acquire key accounting terminology in an exciting forensic hunt for evidence of accounting malpractice. Completion of this section will also put students in the position to discuss in detail the key components of **balance sheets** such as **current assets, accounts payable, accounts receivable** and many more. This section of the unit also examines the use of diplomatic language – breaking bad news – and gives students the chance to identify ways of presenting unpalatable information.

In the *Over to you* section of this unit students get the chance to deal with short legal documents, excerpts from the **Sarbanes-Oxley Act** signed into law after the *Enron* scandal.

For easily digestible short articles explaining key principles behind accounting, see:
http://www.quickmba.com/accounting/

For more information about the various roles and responsibilities within accounting see:
http://www.jobbankusa.com/career_employment/accountants_auditors/job_descriptions_definitions_roles_responsibility.html

For a quick reference on how to understand financial statements see:
http://www.sec.gov/investor/pubs/begfinstmtguide.htm

## Warm-up

Address this warm-up with the whole class: keep the mood upbeat and the pace swift in order to grab your students' attention. Regarding the first question: prompt the students if necessary by asking how many of them think accounting is an exciting subject and how many think that it is easy to study. Allow time for as many students as possible to express their views before moving on.

Turning to the next question, make sure the students understand the expression cooking the books by drawing attention to the cartoon and asking if the accountants depicted look like they're involved in an entirely honest activity. Next, point out to the class that, though many find accounting a dull subject, this question underlines its crucial nature for businesses. Allow a full five minutes for whole-class discussion.

77

# 10 Accounting

> **Mistakes:** can lead to stakeholders in the company – e.g. shareholders, other investors, employees – to believe that the company is more/less profitable than it really is.
> **Poor or fraudulent accounting practice:** is can lead to prosecution, financial penalties, loss of reputation and even jail sentences as well as the loss of jobs and pension funds for employees.

Ask your students to glance over the job descriptions in the margin, then to close their Course Books. Get two or three students to summarize the roles in their own words. Now ask if anyone can offer examples of the type of activities that can be attributed to the roles. Spend a moment collecting suggestions before asking the students to open their Course Books then complete the matching with the class assisting with any vocabulary the students may find tricky.

## Reading: The Enron Story

**1** Carry out this task with the whole class. Explain that the cartoons depict the phrases in question rather literally and encourage your students to shout out their suggestions for matches keeping the mood light-hearted.

> 1 C, 2 D, 3 A, 4 E, 5 B

Explain to your class that the phrases are rather idiomatic than literal in meaning: students may have to think laterally in order to understand them. Ask your students to volunteer their speculations as to the meanings of the expressions in an accounting context gently prodding them in the right direction where necessary so that they arrive at precise definitions. Encourage your students to record the expressions in their vocabulary notebooks.

**2** The students should now work individually to complete the gap-fill exercise. Increase the level of challenge by setting a strict time limit on the exercise before bringing the class back together to check answers.

> 1 number crunching
> 2 massaged the figures
> 3 blew the whistle
> 4 keep an eye on the bottom line
> 5 bean-counters

> **Bookkeeping**
> 1 collecting and filing purchase invoices from suppliers
> 3 recording sales made to customers
> 5 entering figures of sales made in computer program
> 6 obtaining the figures of a business's inventory at end of year
>
> **Accounting**
> 2 establishing rules and methods for determining the effects of financial transactions
> 4 preparing and distributing financial statements
> 7 preparing and submitting tax returns to government
> 8 reviewing and approving end-of-period entries

**3** Tell your students that they will now carry out some important vocabulary groundwork for the reading that will follow. Ask them to work with the person sitting next to them to match the terms to their definitions. As none of the vocabulary in the definitions should present a challenge, students will be able to carry out the matching quite straightforwardly. However, when confirming the correct answers after the matching phase, take time to expand upon the definitions and offer students sample sentences such as those below.

**Suggestions for sample sentences:**
1 Marianne is the *CFO*: she sits on the board and is responsible for all aspects of the company finances.
2 We have an *auditor* coming in next week so let's make sure there are no mistakes in the books.
3 As finance director, Brian Mills has *oversight* of all accounting processes.
4 The *entity* in question, *Millman Sports Wear*, has a net value of $278,000.
5 The *net value* of our premises is $387,000.
6 He's a *CPA*: he should know what he's talking about when it comes to accounting.
7 Reeve's *resignation* from his post as CFO followed accusations of accounting fraud stretching back to 2005.
8 Blair Morgan was sent to prison for four years for his part in the country's largest ever accounting *fraud*.

> 1 f, 2 c, 3 g, 4 b, 5 h, 6 a, 7 e, 8 d

# Accounting 10

**4** Tell your students that they are going to read an article about an accounting news story which was covered widely by the media several years ago. Point out that the terms they have just matched to their definitions all appear in the article. They should now spend a few minutes with the person next to them discussing what an article which features such terms might be about. When they have finished their discussion, bring the class back together and ask students to call out their suggestions about the possible content of the article. Write their suggestions on the board.

As an alternative to letting students scan the article for the answers to all ten questions on their own, you might consider turning this into a more communicative exercise. To do this, divide the students into groups of three or four giving each student roughly equal numbers of questions to work on. The student you judge to be the strongest reader can have an extra question. Distribute each student with questions from the beginning to the end of the list so that they have to scan the entire article for the answers. Make sure that all the questions are being covered.

Students should now scan the article to find the answers to their questions. Remind them that they should have the questions clearly in mind as they read rapidly over the text before arriving at the information they are specifically interested in. They should ignore any unknown vocabulary when doing so. When the students have finished reading, group members should share the information they have gathered with one another. Students should tell each other in as much detail as possible about what they have read. When this stage is over, bring the class back together and refer back to the speculations that the students made about the article before reading it. In instances, where their speculations proved accurate, draw their attention to this and congratulate them. Now, ask a few volunteers to provide the answers to questions which they did not read about themselves. Confirm the correct answers and keep the students in their groups even though they will work individually on the next step.

1. energy and broadband
2. 20,000 people
3. $65 billion
4. Jeffrey Skilling
5. Andy Fastow
6. off-balance sheet transactions (inflating its earnings and hiding debt in partnership constructions)
7. Arthur Andersen
8. Sherron Watkins
9. Securities and Exchange Commission (SEC)
10. conspiracy and fraud

**5** Draw your students' attention to the three questions and ask the groups to spend five minutes discussing them. One member of each group should keep a note of the answers. After the discussion bring the class back together and ask for volunteers to call out answers. Encourage other students to add extra information or to disagree. Allow time for discussion about the third question in particular. You could encourage the discussion by playing devil's advocate and putting questions such as *So, you want more regulatory supervision of accounting practices, right? But isn't that against the spirit of the free market?* Don't forget to confirm the correct answers during the course of discussion.

1. Employees did not only lose their jobs but also their health insurance and retirement funds.
2. There had been no evidence that *Enron* was breaking the law.
3. *Enron* showed that more government oversight is necessary and especially that accounting firms should be subject to strict rules.

Finally, invite the students to call out words from the article they did not understand and write these on the board. Expect to write up *lucrative*, *dubious*, *flattering*, *immanent*, and *serving time*. Don't be tempted to define the words yourself at this stage. Instead, remind students that the meaning of unknown words can often be arrived at by examining the context in which they are used. Taking each word in turn, ask the students to analyze the context it is used in and call out what they think the word means. Offer gentle prodding in the right direction so that students can arrive at the meaning of the words themselves. In the cases where they don't manage to do this, provide your own definitions.

79

# 10 Accounting

## Listening: The world after Enron

### The stuff of headlines

> You may choose to supplement this listening exercise and assist your students in their understanding of the radio interview by using this photocopiable activity.
>
> Pair up your students and give each pair the headlines cut-up on strips of paper. Ask the students to shuffle these and explain that they are fictitious newspaper headlines referring to various points touched upon in the radio interview. Allow your students some moments to read over the headlines, then play the CD track. The students' task is to arrange the headlines in the order that the issues they refer to are mentioned in the radio interview. The students should begin this sorting while listening. However, as the headlines may require some interpretation as to which issues they refer to, allow a few minutes for the pairs to discuss the headlines once the listening phase is over. Confirm the correct order for your students.

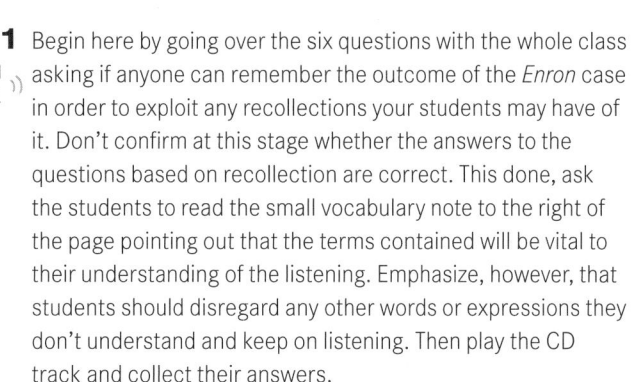

**1** Begin here by going over the six questions with the whole class asking if anyone can remember the outcome of the *Enron* case in order to exploit any recollections your students may have of it. Don't confirm at this stage whether the answers to the questions based on recollection are correct. This done, ask the students to read the small vocabulary note to the right of the page pointing out that the terms contained will be vital to their understanding of the listening. Emphasize, however, that students should disregard any other words or expressions they don't understand and keep on listening. Then play the CD track and collect their answers.

1 Accountants lost their credibility.
2 
- inflate sales figures
- inflate figures for expenses
- record profits for products and services that have not been sold
- record expenses that have not been incurred
- fail to record losses
- fail to disclose negative matters
- make misleading disclosures

3 
- because it had had such a good reputation
- because it was serving both as consultant and auditor to *Enron*
- because it broke the law by shredding *Enron's* documents

4 
- accountancy firms are now accountable to new regulatory body, PCAOB
- accountancy firms can no longer exercise dual role

5 
- Accountants are in high demand.
- Their salaries have risen.

6 
- CEO and CFO are now personally responsible for accuracy of financial reports under Sarbanes-Oxley Act (2002)
- companies must spend more time and money to comply with new standards

**2** Divide your students into groups before playing the listening a second time. After the listening draw their attention to the question giving them between five and ten minutes to discuss it. After the discussion, ask which students feel that enough has been done to prevent further accounting scandals and which think that the measures taken fall short of preventing history repeating itself. Ask the students to volunteer some of the reasons behind their opinions and note these in two columns on the board assisting with formulation where necessary. Congratulate your students on a fruitful discussion.

### Business Skills

## Talking about balance sheets: Using the right terms

**1** Tell your students that they are now going to get the opportunity to sort some key accounting terms under the correct headings before moving on to look at a balance sheet. Point out how the exercise works by drawing attention to the example which has already been entered on the mind map and give the students five minutes to complete the mind map with the terms for the box. While they are doing so, draw the mind map as it appears in the Course Book on the board. After the allotted time, bring the class back together to collect answers. Do this either by taking the words in the order that they appear in the box and asking students where they placed these or ask students to take a category from the mind map and say what they included in it. As they call out their answers, write these into the mind map on the board. Should a student place an item in the wrong place, ask others to suggest where it should go. When the correct answers have been confirmed and the mind map on the board is complete, encourage students to choose at least five items from it which they think will be useful to them and to record these in their vocabulary notes.

# Accounting 10

## Mind map: Accounting

- **Types of financial statements**
  - balance sheet
  - cash flow statement
  - profit and loss account

- **Purpose of accounts**
  - monitor activity
  - provide information
  - reduce chance of fraud
  - guarantee transparency

- **Balance sheet items**
  - Assets
    - office equipment
    - property
    - debtor
    - bank accounts
    - raw materials
  - Liabilities
    - creditor
    - bank loans

- **People at work**
  - auditor
  - bookkeeper
  - chief accounting officer
  - chief financial officer

---

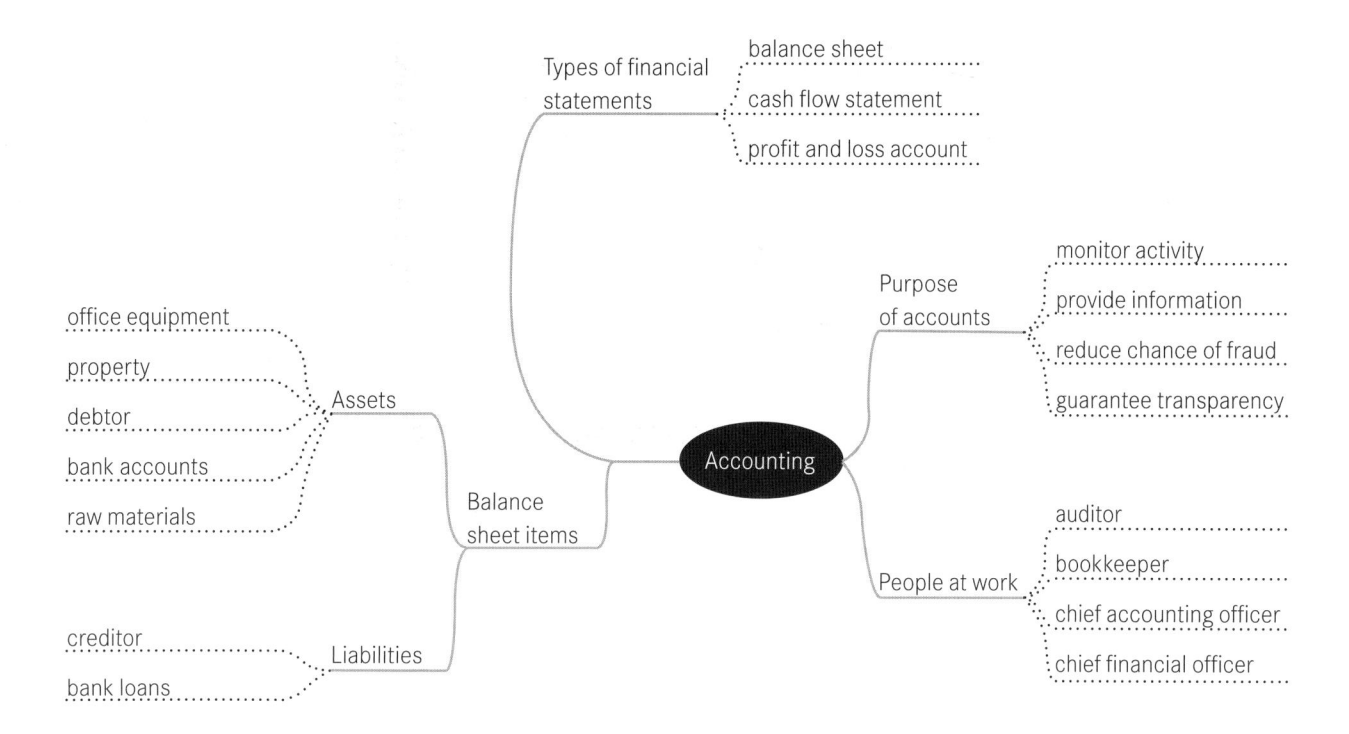

**2** It will probably be worth quickly revising how numbers are expressed in English before moving onto this listening here. In order to do this, point out to the class that all the figures expressed on the balance sheet are in millions, then pick students at random to say them. This done, ask the students to speculate about the kinds of difficulties someone in Jim's position might have with accounting. Clearly, given his arts background, Jim may find it difficult to understand the basic concepts and terminology of accounting. Confirm that the listening will feature the kind of simple explanations that Jim requires to understand the company's balance sheet. Point out to the students that the way they listen to the CD track should nevertheless be aimed at obtaining the figures currently missing from the balance sheet. They should not get bogged down with terminology they don't understand.

After playing the CD, collect answers by asking volunteers to come to the board and write the figures up: they should say them at the same time.

Note that several of the terms which students will have to define in exercise 4 have been included in the listening to make their job later a little easier.

| 1 | 105,000 | 5 | 60,000 |
| 2 | -18,000 | 6 | 60,000 |
| 3 | 132,000 | 7 | 12,000 |
| 4 | 7,500 | 8 | 72,000 |

**3** Split your students into pairs to tackle this exercise the purpose of which is two-fold: to acquaint students with a range of technical expressions and to allow them to demonstrate their expertise in analyzing a balance sheet. Be sure to draw upon the students' expertise when it comes to the latter task and allow them to show what they have learned on their accounting course.

- The fact that the value of its assets had almost doubled between Year 1 and Year 3 and that its total assets exceeded by far its total liabilities would lead you to believe the company was performing well.
- The beauty of the fraud was that there was no indication that the company would be bankrupt in less than a year as it could not be detected in the balance sheet.

**4** You may consider playing CD track 15 again at this point as several of the terms are defined in the listening. Before you do so, point out to your students that they are to match the terms highlighted on the balance sheet with the definitions on the following page. If they listen to the CD, they should have familiarized themselves with the expressions they are interested in beforehand. Collect answers around the class before advising students to record any terms which are new to them in their vocabulary notes.

# 10 Accounting

1. all of the money owed to the business
   **net receivables**
2. the part of the profit not paid out as dividends, but kept by the company to be reinvested or be used to pay debts
   **retained earnings**
3. the net amount of capital received from investors
   **total stockholder equity**
4. the value of intangible assets such as a strong brand or company reputation. On a balance sheet, this can refer to the purchase of a brand name or the acquisition of a company with a good reputation
   **goodwill**
5. the goods or raw materials held in stock
   **inventory**
6. the portion of shares that a company does not want to put on the market
   **treasury stock**
7. the deduction of capital expenses over a specific period of time, usually over the asset's life
   **amortization**
8. stock owned in a corporation that has a higher claim on the assets and earnings than common stock
   **preferred stock**
9. money the company owes but can only repay at some point in the future
   **deferred long term liability charges**
10. money that the company owes to its creditors at the present time
    **current liabilities**

## Diplomacy: Breaking the bad news

**1** Warm up for this exercise by holding up the Course Book and pointing at the photographs of Susan and John telling students who they are and what the relationship between them is. Say that Susan has some bad news for John and encourage students to speculate as to what that might be: the unit so far will have given them some food for thought about accounting malpractice with which they can nourish their speculations. Write their suggestions on the board.

Now play the first conversation so that students can find out if their speculations proved correct. Collect answers in open class.

Conversation 1
- Susan has discovered irregularities in the company's accounts.
- John reacts with objections, excuses and a threat.

**2** Now make it clear to students that they are going to hear what amounts to the same conversation again but that, on this occasion, Susan's approach is different. They must listen and say in which ways it differs from the first listening. Encourage the students to give you examples from the listening to back up their opinions.

Conversation 2
- Susan is much more diplomatic, thanks to her use of softeners and tentative language.
  She also uses "first person-messages", e.g. *I'm very concerned about ...*

**3** Ask your students to listen to the second conversation again in order to complete the gaps. Given that they have already listened to this track, they will probably complete the sentences without difficulty. However, you may consider pausing the CD in order that students who are less confident can note down the answers correctly. Check answers in open class.

Round off by asking the students to underline the words or phrases which they consider to have the greatest softening effect on Susan's statements. They should certainly underline *unfortunately*, *don't quite*, *not quite as* and *there is the possibility*.

1. John, <u>as you know</u>, we've been reviewing your financial statements for last year and, <u>unfortunately</u>, there are a number of figures that <u>don't quite add up</u>.
2. Yes. <u>I'm sorry to say</u> that that the figure for earnings is not supported by the other documents we've had access to.
3. But it's <u>not quite as successful</u> as the figures in the financial statements.
4. Well, <u>there is the possibility</u> that it is <u>a deliberate misrepresentation</u> but we <u>can also assume that it was just</u> an error.
5. As an external auditor, I <u>have no choice but to insist</u> the company restates the original financial report.
6. But the earnings figure is clearly off by at least $5m. <u>I'm very concerned about that</u>.

82

## Company Case: **A back office in India**

Begin by ensuring that your students understand the meaning of *back office*: the term refers to administrative functions of a business which are not immediately pertinent to the services or products it sells. Ask your students to get into groups and set them the initial task of scan reading the text in order to decide the meaning of *outlet*, *onshore*, *offshore* and *royalties* from the context they are used in. Give them a few minutes to confer in their groups as to definitions then bring the class back together to collect and confirm answers.

Students should then read the text again more closely to answer the first four questions. Collect and confirm answers in open class.

**Factors that could make an offshore arrangement difficult for the company:**
- time difference (9.5 hrs to EST)
- physical distance (so far F&A operations have been in-house)
- restaurant business is paper-based
- cultural differences
- language problems (difficulties in understanding Indian accent)

**Potential risks:**
- data security
- professionalism of foreign staff

**Factors to consider in choosing service provider:**
- knowledge of restaurant industry
- professional reputation
- familiarity with software systems already in use at *Hacienda Heaven*

**Measures that could reduce potential problems:**
- staff visits
- liaison officer (from Indian provider) who is permanently present at headquarters
- new 800 number for outlet managers, connecting them directly with the service provider in India

Next, give the groups 20 minutes to discuss and decide upon which course of action they would recommend that *Hacienda Heaven* take. Ask the students to spend the last ten minutes structuring their recommendations in presentation form: each groups' presentation should include an introduction, a main body which makes clear the rationales behind the recommendations and a conclusion.

Allow a few minutes for the other students to comment upon the recommendations after each group have given their presentation. Congratulate your students on their efforts and explain that the case study is based on the experience of *Church Chicken*, which outsourced its accounting operations to India and introduced the measures mentioned in the text.

## Over to you

### Skills: Paraphrasing

1. *Enron's* bankruptcy resulted in unemployment for its 20,000 former employees.
2. It was a publicly traded company (...) whose shares were considered a blue chip investment not only in the U.S. but around the world.
3. These were declared as independent partnerships and used in off-balance sheet transactions to conceal *Enron's* debt.
4. (...) these had not reported the irregularities, either as a result of incompetence or collusion with the *Enron* management.
5. Jeffrey Skilling resigned – allegedly for personal reasons.
6. (...) admitting that it has been inflating its earnings (...)
7. All three men were found guilty of the offences (...)

### Web research: Becoming an accountant

Regarding the second question, ensure that your students understand that they should combine the search terms from the Course Book along with the countries in order to obtain information specific to each country.

### Web research: Investigating fraud

Advise your students that this website contains articles about recent accounting scandals which they can use as a springboard to their investigations:
http://www.corporatenarc.com/accountingscandals.php

# 10 Accounting

## Reading: Legal documents

Prepare your students for this reading by pointing out that, when it comes to legalese such as this, the "devil is in the detail": they will have to read closely in order to understand. Point out that even native speakers of English would have to read over such texts slowly and carefully. Stress that, though the sentences in the texts appear long and dense, they are often, in fact, lists in sentence form. Careful reading will reveal that the ideas contained within the texts, while expressed at some length, are ultimately not difficult to understand.

**1** The subject is the subordinate clause *'Whoever knowingly, with the intent to retaliate, takes any action harmful to any person, including interference with the lawful employment or livelihood of any person, for providing to a law enforcement officer any truthful information relating to the commission or possible commission of any federal offence …'*
The verb is *'shall be fined, (shall be) imprisoned'*

**2**
- the means of earning the money you need to exist
  **livelihood**
- the act of perpetrating a crime
  **commission**
- an illegal act
  **offence**
- the division of a legal text or statute
  **title**
- a person working for the government with the job of ensuring that laws are observed
  **law enforcement officer**

**3** The person could be fined <u>and</u> sent to prison for 10 years.

**4** The subject is *'Whoever knowingly alters, destroys, mutilates, conceals, covers up, falsifies, or makes a false entry in any record, document, or tangible object with the intent to impede, obstruct, or influence the investigation or proper administration of any matter within the jurisdiction of any department or agency of the United States or any case filed under title 11, or in relation to or contemplation of any such matter or case …'*

**5**
- the act of carrying out a function
  **administration**
- to change in a fraudulent way
  **falsify**
- to remove or damage a part of something
  **mutilate**
- authority or control
  **jurisdiction**
- material, capable of being touched
  **tangible**

**6** The punishment for dishonest accountants is even harsher, as they could be fined and imprisoned for 20 years.

## Writing: Blowing the whistle

Invite your students to send you their letters so that you can comment upon them and return them before or at the next class. Target your corrections and comments at the students' use of the phrases provided in the language box and in the *Useful expressions* list at the back of the Course Book.

# 11 Rapidly developing economies

**Self Study**

**Vocabulary**
- Word families: Frequently used terminology
- Verbs and nouns of change with prepositions
- Word partnerships highlighting economic facts and trends

**Grammar**
- Creating flow through linking words
- Mixed tenses in graph descriptions
- The Crystal Ball: Speculation and prediction

**Skills**
- Adjectives and adverbs describing change
- Describing change
- Summarizing information from a graph

**Reading**
- Understanding a country report
- Keywords in a country report

## At a glance

At the end of this unit your students will be in no doubt about the kind of globalized world economy they will be going to work in. Any assumptions they may make about the continuing dominance of Western economies in the future will be challenged by the developments outlined in this unit.

The unit's study of rapidly developing economies takes the **BRIC** countries (Brazil, Russia, India and China) as its focus. The significance of this grouping lies in the fact that many economists believe that the four countries' economies combined will become more important than current major economic powers. The fact that the strengths of the four countries, as well as the challenges facing them, are so diverse makes the BRIC phenomenon all the more fertile in terms of its potential to generate classroom discussion.

The range of the unit's vocabulary takes in economic indices including **gross domestic product (GDP)** and **purchasing power parity per capita**, as well as other vocabulary key to any discussion of economic development including **exchange rate, foreign direct investment (FDI), commodity, surplus** and **frugal engineering**.

The unit's *Business Skills* section is the closely linked area of describing trends and developments. Students will encounter the full range of language to enable them to discuss economic development. They will also receive ample opportunity to put the language into practice analyzing graphs charting the economic development of the BRIC countries. The *Company Case* presents an interesting study of the intercultural implications of doing business in a rapidly developing economy for a Western company.

For further information on the BRICs countries see this presentation from the *World Bank*: http://siteresources.worldbank.org/INTRUSSIANFEDERATION/147270-1109938296415/21077781/BRIC_Eng.pdf

The four-part *BBC* radio documentary featured on this website provides a solid and entertaining overview of the issues raised by rapidly developing economies: http://news.bbc.co.uk/2/hi/programmes/documentary_archive/4287124.stm

## Warm-up

Begin by telling your students that they are going to get a chance to test their knowledge of the global economy by completing the quiz. Pre-teach the terms *gross domestic product*, *biannual*, *creditworthiness*, *subsidiary* and *purchasing power parity per capita*. Then ask the class to do the quiz.

When everyone has finished, ask the students to check their scores and read the comments about them. Ask students whether they have already taken any courses in economics and if they have any other experience concerning economics which they were able to draw upon during the quiz.

Now turn your students' attention to the question at the bottom of the page asking students to share their insight with the class. Provoke discussion by putting questions such as *So, what are the positive implications of rapidly developing economies for the advanced industrial world?* and *Will there be any good news for advanced economies in the long run?*

The students might suggest the following influences:
- Rapidly developing economies provide opportunities for the investment of Western capital.
- They can potentially absorb increasing amounts of Western industrial exports.
- Their manufacturing exports to the West can challenge the position of Western manufacturers in their own markets.
- Rapidly developing economies can attract the off-shoring of jobs away from the West.

85

# 11 Rapidly developing economies

## Reading: The BRIC countries

**1** Before asking students to fill in the mind map ask your students to explain the difference between *macro-economic* and *micro-economic*.

- *Macro-economic* refers to the performance and structure of an entire economy be that at the regional, national or global level
- *Micro-economic* refers to the study of individual units of an economy be these individuals, households or companies

Ask your students to complete the mind map. While they are doing so, either sketch the mind map onto the board or project a slide onto the board using a beamer. Bring the class back together and collect answers. You may decide to expand the exercise by asking students if they can think of any other factors which fit under the four determiners. Additionally, ask them for examples of each of the factors. Enter their suggestions into the mind map.

Now draw the students' attention to the other category (*supporting factors*) of the mind map and ask the pairs to spend five minutes speculating as to what a list of supporting factors might include. Collect answers in open class and be prepared to beef up the students' combined list with a few suggestions of your own.

Round off this stage by encouraging your students to discuss instances of economic failure at the national level that they might know of from their economics studies. How did the factors cited in the mind map interrelate to create economic crisis in these instances? Ask students who display particularly detailed knowledge to model the process of economic disintegration in the form of flow charts on the board, i. e. *weak political institutions → corruption and bad policy making → macroeconomic instability → business failure → unemployment,* etc.

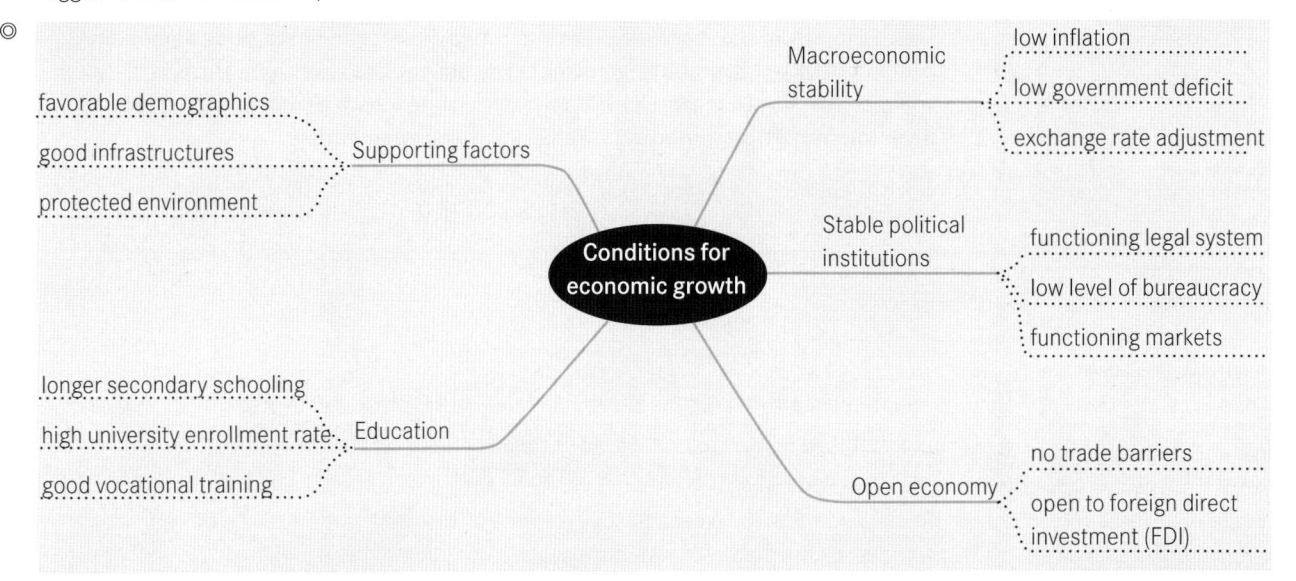

**Mind map: Conditions for economic growth**

- Supporting factors
  - favorable demographics
  - good infrastructures
  - protected environment
- Macroeconomic stability
  - low inflation
  - low government deficit
  - exchange rate adjustment
- Stable political institutions
  - functioning legal system
  - low level of bureaucracy
  - functioning markets
- Education
  - longer secondary schooling
  - high university enrollment rate
  - good vocational training
- Open economy
  - no trade barriers
  - open to foreign direct investment (FDI)

**2** Point out the importance of this exercise by explaining that understanding the terms will assist the students in the reading exercise. Invite the pairs to match the terms to their definitions.

If you judge that your students can complete the matching swiftly, turn it into a quiz. The students should remain in their pairs and you should play the role of quiz master, reading out each term in turn. Students should confer quickly with their partners. When they have agreed on a match they should spring to their feet and provide their answer. If it's right they get a point, if it's wrong open the question back up to the other pairs. Continue until all the terms have been dealt with and congratulate the winners.

1 b, 2 c, 3 e, 4 d, 5 h, 6 a, 7 g, 8 i, 9 f

**3** Put pairs together to form groups of four. Inject structure into the students' discussions by writing the following categories on the board and asking the students to address them in their discussions: *population*, *GDP*, *trade deficit*, *political system* and *current political orientation*. Give the students five minutes to pool their collective knowledge about conditions in each of the four countries. When the five minutes are up, ask one group to summarize what it knows about China, the next group about India and so on. After each group has finished, invite supplementary information from other students. Summarize the information provided by the students in four small mind maps in each corner of the board. Leave this information on the board as you can return to it during exercise 6. Your students should remain in their groups of four for the reading exercise.

If you want to periodically refresh your own knowledge about economic developments in the BRIC countries, you might want to try out the following link:
http://www.economist.com/markets-data/

# Rapidly developing economies  11

**4** Explain to your students that each group member is going to read a text about one of the countries in order to be able to answer the questions of other group members about it.

Invite your students to choose a country and begin reading now. Encourage those that finish before other team members to work on the formulation of their questions ensuring that they are correct. Once each group member has finished reading and thought of five questions, the students should take turns to summarize what they have read. Point out that each student has a maximum of two minutes for their summaries after which the other students should put their questions.

Listen in on the groups' discussions, paying particular attention to the formulation of the questions. Should you pick up on any mistakes, take note of them for later self-correction by the students. When the discussion is over, bring the class back together and invite a student who did not read about, for instance, Brazil to summarize what they have learned as a result of the group discussion. When they have finished, invite other students to contribute further points. Deal with the other three countries in the same way before writing any mistakes that were made during the group discussions on the board. Invite the class to correct them.

**5** You may want to offer your students the chance to read about another country at this stage, if so assign each group member another text to read and ask them to find the expressions which match the illustrations and complete the gapped sentences. Confirm that students have answered correctly in open class.

Now invite questions about vocabulary by asking students to read out words they are unsure of and writing these on the board. Before providing your own explanations, ask if other students can explain individual words or expressions. Be ready to answer questions about *surge*, *hike*, *endemic violation* and *soared*.

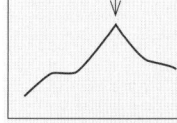

**Brazil:** The level of foreign direct investment inflows reached a record high of US$34.6.billion in 2007.

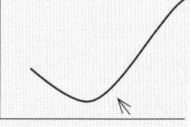

**Russia:** Despite the difficult business environment, foreign direct investment (FDI) has picked up in recent years.

**Brazil:** Its population is young, but its birth rate and mortality rate are both decreasing.

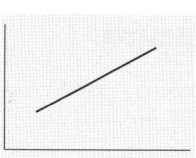

**China:** Enrollment in universities has gone up.
China's economy grew by an average of 10% a year between 1981 and 2007.

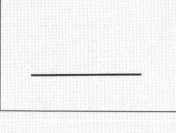

**China:** Consumer price inflation has remained relatively low over the last years.

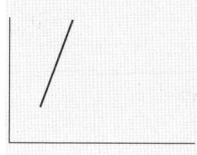

**India:** Although consumer price inflation fell to roughly 4% in the early 2000s, it has accelerated again. FDI inflows used to be very low but jumped to $24.5 billion in 2007/08.

**6** The groups should now consider this question. Encourage them to organize their results under two headings: *Reasons for growth* and *Room for improvement*. After allowing the students ten minutes for their discussions bring the class back together and ask the students to call out the results of their reading. Consolidate this information by using it to complete the mind maps which you put on the board before.

**Brazil**
Reasons for growth: government policy between 1994 and the present, large and developed agriculture, mining, manufacturing and service sectors, floating exchange rate, surge in exports, high and increasing FDI
Room for improvement: complex legal system, declining birth rate and ageing population, school education system, infrastructure and environmental protection

**Russia**
Reasons for growth: rich in natural resources, strong currency, booming domestic consumption, growing FDI
Room for improvement: high inflation rates, under-funded education and infrastructure, demographic challenges, bureaucracy, legal system

**India**
Reasons for growth: increasing FDI, well-developed service sector
Room for improvement: corruption, bureaucracy, inadequate legal system, demographic challenges, limited natural resources, high consumer price inflation

**China**
Reasons for growth: large reserves of natural resources, enormous labor force, burgeoning exports, booming FDI, low consumer price inflation, impressive infrastructural improvements
Room for improvement: dependence on oil imports, water shortages resulting from intensive agriculture, low private consumption, under-valued currency, quality of education

# 11 Rapidly developing economies

## Role-play: Investor's choice

Split your students into new groups of five asking those students who read about India to be India's representatives, the experts on China to represent China, etc. Should you have a group of less than five students, drop a country file from the role-play. Double up students for some of the roles if you have a group of more than five students. Rather than have students play the role of a British investor, you may decide that they take the role of an investor from their own countries of origin. This may make it easier for students to "get into" their roles.

Now draw the students' attention to their roles' language boxes. Explain that they should aim to use at least three of the phrases in the course of the role-play. Next form five groups made up of investors and representatives from each of the countries. Tell the investors that they have five minutes to work on the formulation of their questions. Investors may be assisted in comparing information from the four countries – and in presenting their final decisions to the class – by a table. Offer the following table as an example and encourage the students to fill it in during their discussions:

|  | Brazil | China | India | Russia |
| --- | --- | --- | --- | --- |
| Population |  |  |  |  |
| Size of economy |  |  |  |  |
| Political climate |  |  |  |  |
| Legal system |  |  |  |  |
| Café retail market |  |  |  |  |

Explain to the country representatives that their five-minute task is to brainstorm as many arguments as possible to present the market conditions in their country in a positive way. While the groups are working on developing their questions and arguments, circulate assisting with formulation and suggesting a few arguments of your own should the students find it hard to come up with any. Once this preparatory phase is complete, put the students into their groups for the role-play and give them 15 minutes to carry it out.

Listen in on the role-plays taking note of any particularly well-structured arguments and mistakes that you might want to pick up on at the end. The role-play over, give the investors a few minutes to work individually to reach their decisions. During this time, work with the other students and cite some of the arguments that you picked up on during the role-play that you were most impressed with.

Finally, call upon the investors to take it in turns to report their decisions and their thinking behind them. Congratulate students on their efforts and invite comments from the other students. Would they have reached similar decisions; if not, what would they have decided and why?

## Listening: Tectonic shifts in the global economy

**1** Point out to your students that the vocabulary covered in the first exercise is crucial to their understanding of the listening. Give them two to three minutes to complete the matching before checking answers in open class.

1 c, 2 a, 3 b, 4 d

**2** Tell your students that they will need to bear the points in the box on the right of the page in mind when listening to the radio program. Give them a few moments to absorb the points before playing the track.

Given the length of the listening, you may decide to break it into two parts. Should you choose to do so, pause the CD after the discussion about the *FT Global 500* list and the phrase … *there are other players like Lenovo, a Chinese computer maker*, and ask students to compare the notes they have made so far with the person sitting next to them. After a few moments let the students listen to the remainder of the CD track. Round off by confirming the answers for the class.

**globality** – a radically competitive environment in which everyone from everywhere competes for everything
**reasons for change** – the lowering of trade barriers, accessible investment banks and accounting firms, talent from everywhere can work anywhere
**the FT Global 500 list** – between 2006 and 2008 the number of companies from BRIC countries quadrupled from 15 to 62
**frugal engineering** – adapting to customers' needs in developing economies and making more out of less
**new business model** – Western companies need to adopt new business models which are appropriate to the markets they want to operate in
**multinationals (opportunities and strengths)** – Western companies maintain their strong lead in management skills, marketing and R&D and are leveraging this to take advantage of opportunities in developing economies

**3** You might consider setting this writing task as homework. Invite your students to email their summaries to you. You should comment upon and return these in the next lesson.

# Rapidly developing economies 11

**Business Skills**

## Describing trends: Economic growth

**1** Begin here by asking which type of graphs are shown on page 108 and introduce the word *line graph*. Allow the class some moments to read the instructions, then ensure that the students understand what they are to do by asking two or three of them to summarize the aim of the exercise in their own words.

Before playing the listening, point out the importance of the students attempting to identify the graphs which are being described without necessarily knowing or understanding all of the vocabulary used. There is undoubtedly much vocabulary which may well be new to students: however, tell them that they will get a chance to examine this in the next exercise. Play the CD track and check answers in open class.

1 b, 2 b

**2** If you have a class of rather able students, you may consider asking them to attempt the gap exercise without listening to the CD again. If you choose to do so, light-heartedly tell the class that you don't expect them to remember everything but that it will be interesting to see how much one can absorb from a listening even when one's attention is directed elsewhere. Play the CD track again so students can check their answers.

Round off by asking students to say which gapped words mean to increase suddenly and dramatically (*rocketed*) and to drop suddenly and dramatically (*plummeted*).

| | |
|---|---|
| 1 rocketed to, in, from, in | 5 plummeted by, to |
| 2 gradually, dramatically, a low of | 6 unsteady, low of |
| | 7 in, of, to |
| 3 steady, in | 8 has declined, in |
| 4 has fallen | |

### Describing trends card game

Prepare your students for exercise 3 by asking them to play this card game. Copy and cut out two sets of phrase cards and two sets of graph cards for each group of four students.

Split your students into their groups and give each one set of phrase cards which the students should spread on the table in front of them. Their first task is to sort the phrases into groups: do they represent growth, decline or stability? Allow just two minutes for this before checking answers with the class. Next, invite your students to explore the nuanced differences between some of the phrases by asking individual students to draw a *sharp increase*, a *dramatic increase* and so forth on line graphs on the board. Keep the tone of this light-hearted and ask other students to try their hand at drawing the required graphs. Point out, however, that as the application of such language is rather subjective, there are no hard and fast rules as to how a *dramatic fall*, for example, differs from *plummeted*.

Your students are now ready to play the game. Hand out the other sets of phrase cards and two graph card sets to each group. The students should keep these separate but shuffle both sets thoroughly. Each student is dealt a hand of five graph cards: the phrase cards are placed face down in the middle of the table.

The game proceeds as follows. The first player takes a card from the pile and decides whether the phrase on it can be used to describe the highlighted section of any of the graphs in their hand. If this is possible, the player must form a sentence about the relevant graph using the phrase – for instance, *Imports increased dramatically between 2003 –2008* – and may then place the phrase and graph cards on the table. If this is not possible, the player places the phrase card at the bottom of the pile on the table and continues into the next round with their five graph cards. It is possible that a student will be in the lucky position of having two cards with the same graph in their hand: if the phrase they pick can be applied to this, both graph cards can be laid down. The next player now takes their turn and so on. The winner is the first player to get rid of all the graph cards from their hand as described: the other players should continue, however, until all the graph cards have been played out.

**3** Put your students into pairs ensuring that they know who will be *Student A* and *Student B*. Tell them that their aim here is not only to describe the graphs to their partners so that they might accurately draw them. They should also try to use as much of the vocabulary for talking about trends that they have learned as possible. To this end, draw the students' attention to the language box on the right of the page allowing them a few moments to study it in order to refresh their memories.

While the students are describing the graphs to one another, circulate and listen in for mistakes in the use of the target language (i.e. expressions for describing trends). Take a note of this so that you can feed it back to the students. Allow your students some time to self-correct by comparing their graphs with those in the Course Book, then write up any mistakes you want to highlight and invite the class to correct them.

89

# 11 Rapidly developing economies

## Describing trends: Comparing economic growth

**1** Divide your students into small groups for this exercise. Ensure that the students understand their task by asking them to summarize it briefly in their own words. Before they begin their discussion about the two line graphs, remind the students that they should try to use as much of the language for talking about trends as possible. Allow between five and ten minutes for the group discussions, then tell the students that they will get a chance to check their answers in the following reading exercise.

**2** Make it clear that the students are to read this short text in the first instance in order to compare what it says with their own analysis of the graph on page 109. Allow them a few minutes to read, then ask the groups to work together to identify any discrepancies between what they decided during their earlier discussion and what the text says.

Round off this stage by bringing the class back together and asking the students if there were any aspects of the relative fortunes of the U.S. and German economies which they found surprising or particularly interesting. Finally, turn to the question of which periods the graph might be split up into. As this is largely a matter of subjective interpretation allow enough time for several students to describe how they would split the graph up.

**3** You may choose to have students complete this exercise either on their own – the activity would work well as a piece of homework or, alternatively, you might turn it into a whole-class, collaborative activity. If you opt for the latter approach, draw the table up on the board and invite students to read the text again and call out the words they identify as they come upon them, saying in which column of the table they should go. The virtue of this approach is that it provides an opportunity for short discussions about the meanings of the terms during which confusions can be cleared up and meanings properly established. Complete the table on the board and ask the students if they can identify any terms which, while describing movement, do not necessarily describe an upward or downward movement: they might identify *fluctuate*. Round off the activity by giving students the chance to copy the results of their collaboration into the table in their Course Books.

| Verbs | | Nouns | |
|---|---|---|---|
| upward movement | downward movement | upward movement | downward movement |
| recover | plummet | reach a peak | drop |
| improve | shrink | | decrease |
| go up | fall | | decline |
| | | | contraction |

## Writing: Comparing economic trends

**1** Ask the students to consider the checklist and decide which points should be applied when writing up descriptions of trends depicted in graphs. Allow five minutes for this discussion before bringing the class back together. Then ask students to return to the text at the top of the page to find examples of the advice provided in the checklist.

**Not correct:**
- by describing the development year by year
- by using short sentences
- by using strong metaphors *(there might be some exceptions)*

**2** Pair off your students and tell them that they can now complete an extended piece of writing describing the trends indicated by the graph at the bottom of the page. Draw their attention to the term *GDP per capita* and ask students to define it: *GDP per capita is calculated by dividing a country's GDP by its population*. Now ask the pairs to discuss the graph using as much of the language for describing trends which they have learned as possible. During the course of this discussion listen in on the discussions taking note of any mistakes you want to highlight before the students move on to the writing stage.

Now set the scene for the students' writing. What they are to produce is, in effect, a briefing paper. Such papers are frequently produced within companies as a preliminary to making important commercial decisions. As such, the paper should be as clear, concise and forcefully argued as possible. In order to achieve this, the students should refer to the checklist in the course of their writing. Ensure that the students understand that their briefing should include a comparison of growth rates in the BRIC countries before concluding with a set of recommendations. Clearly, the graph provides material for a fairly long piece of writing. However, explain that it would be entirely realistic for a word limit to be applied to such documents to render them easily digestible for busy readers. Set a word limit of five hundred words which the students should stay within.

# 11 Rapidly developing economies

## Company Case: A multinational's approach to the Chinese market

Prepare your students for the case study by telling them that they are going to read about a Western cosmetics company which encountered problems selling its products in the Chinese market. Ask students to speculate about the nature of the problems that the company might have encountered. Write their suggestions on the board before asking them to read the case study.

After they have read the text, ask several students to recount what the text says: stop a student after s/he has explained a few points and ask the next to pick up where their classmate left off.

Having completed this, ask the class to read the text again. They should now underline any words they don't understand. Before moving on to the discussion stage, allow a few minutes for your students to ask questions about vocabulary: in particular, you should be prepared to explain *endorsement* and *waiver*.

Now split your class into four groups. The groups should consider each of the questions in turn but should be prepared to present their findings for one of the questions to the rest of the class: they should work on this presentation collaboratively but elect one group member to deliver it. Ensure that each group knows which question it should present on. The groups should spend a few minutes preparing this presentation but make it clear that they should not spend unnecessary time on this at the expense of the remaining questions.

When the group discussion is over, bring the class back together asking groups to present the results of their discussions. After each presentation, invite comment and supplementary information from the other groups. Allocate more time for the discussion of the final question, allowing all the groups the chance to elaborate on their "relaunch" plan for the company's products on the Chinese market.

1. In general one can say that *Cosmo* underestimated the powerful influence of the Chinese government, the massive media coverage of this incident in- and outside China as well as the forceful reactions of the Chinese consumers.
   China is a country with a long-standing and successful tradition of healing ailments and illnesses with natural remedies and techniques. People are slightly wary of chemical substances.
   Mistakes in detail:
   - They denied the allegations made by the Chinese testing institute.
   - They didn't do any second testing in order to show that the company was taking the official testing results seriously.
   - They linked their refund policy to certain conditions which partly violated Chinese law.
   - They didn't accept any mistakes on the part of the company.
   - They showed arrogance by not apologizing to the Chinese consumer.
   - They destroyed the trust between the company and its customers by being stingy in their refund policy.
2. *Cosmo's* situation is tricky because admitting that the KBS product line in China could be harmful to health would certainly have led to brand damage in the other East Asian countries and a series of legal disputes there. Also admitting to having sold a faulty product would have damaged *Cosmo's* other (sub-) brands.
3. *Cosmo* shouldn't have claimed that the government test results were wrong; they should have used an unrestricted refund policy and they could have launched a good-will marketing campaign.
4. They could monitor the production of KBS products more carefully; they could try to reduce the levels of the chemical substances; they could practice a more open policy, i.e. informing the consumers as fully as possible; they could react to complaints in a more generous way, e.g. apart from giving a full refund they could invite customers to their production facilities.

# 11 Rapidly developing economies

## Over to you

### Web research: New economic developments

Direct your students' research to the following website which is provided by the *World Bank* and includes a comprehensive, country-by-country breakdown of key economic and societal data. Your students should choose the countries they are interested in under *Country Profiles*:
http://data.worldbank.org/country

### Writing: Assessing investment opportunities

Remind your students of the analysis and recommendation they completed in exercise 2 on page 110 and point out that they have a further opportunity to practice the target language here. Advise them to refer again to the checklist on page 110 and the *Useful expressions* list on page 167 when writing their report. Ask them to keep their reports within a four-hundred word limit and invite your students to email their work to you so that you can return it with your comments.

### Reading: Products for those at the bottom of the pyramid

1 Encourage your students to read the article by pointing out the interesting approach to market research and product development discussed in it: this has evolved to meet the commercial needs of companies - as well as the needs of the people they are selling to - in low income countries.

2  1  **BOP:** some four billion people around the world who eke out a living on about two U.S. dollars a day
Important for businesses: money can be made by developing and marketing products for those at the bottom of the pyramid
   2  Products for those at the bottom of the pyramid not only have to be cheap but they have to meet the specific needs of the target group.
**PUR:** P&G used NGOs as partners who took over sales and distribution using their expertise and so *PUR* became a commercially viable product.

**Electricité de France:** instead of donating solar panels or fuel powered generators they assist people in setting up their own little energy businesses; the effect is that these people have an income and feel responsible for keeping the energy supply going.
**Essilor India:** because of limited infrastructure and people mobility in rural areas the company set up mobile eye specialist surgeries which were used to bring the service of eye examination and treatment as well as the manufacture and delivery of spectacles to people's doorsteps.

3 Companies should come up with product innovations which raise the standard of living of the developing countries without damaging the environment.

### Language work: Word combinations and phrasal verbs

Remind your students of the importance of learning vocabulary in the word combinations - or collocations - that it frequently occurs in. Emphasize that this approach is of particular use when it comes to learning phrasal verbs where the addition of a preposition or adverb alters the meaning of the original verb. Point out that all of the collocations and phrasal verbs here are to be found in the article. Encourage the students to complete these two exercises by telling them that you will review the answers at the next class.

1  1  d, eke out
   2  e, address needs
   3  f, hold potential for
   4  g, meet the needs
   5  i, close down
   6  b, ease the pressure on
   7  a, off the grid
   8  c, raise awareness
   9  h, consumption patterns

2  1  address the needs     6  consumption patterns
   2  close down            7  holds, potential for
   3  eke out               8  meets, needs
   4  raise, awareness      9  off the grid
   5  ease the pressure on

# 12 Starting a business

### Self Study

**Vocabulary**
- Starting a business: key expressions
- Getting a business going
- Starting a business: legal vocabulary

**Grammar**
- Modals: Rules for different forms of companies in Britain
- Tense practice: tell me how it all began
- Future tenses in a business plan

**Skills**
- Putting together the executive summary
- Writing an executive summary I
- Writing an executive summary II

**Reading**
- Dealing with unfamiliar words
- Understanding an executive summary

## At a glance

This final unit of *Career Express Business English B2* is designed to get your students thinking about the prospects of them going into the world of business and considering **entrepreneurship**. The unit examines the role universities play in fostering entrepreneurial spirit among students as well as discussing what the key factors in successful entrepreneurship are. It also affords students the opportunity to assess if they are made of the right stuff to start their own businesses by encouraging them to examine their personal responses to issues such as **working conditions**, **responsibilities**, **motivation** and **self-management** in the context of running a **start-up** business.

The unit takes a close look at what is included in a **business plan** such as the **company**, **market analysis** and **management summaries** as well as the **sales forecast**, and gives students the opportunity to assess the viability of a realistic business plan.

The unit's *Business Skills* section then moves on to consider the **executive summary** before examining terminology for describing the various legal forms of companies such as **sole trader**, **partnership** and **limited liability**. The *Company Case* consists of an exciting exercise in troubleshooting for a successful start-up which has run into problems managing its brand image.

For brief articles about starting a business which will help to warm you up for teaching this unit see:
http://www.score.org

This U.K.-based website provides a comprehensive list of the activities that need to be undertaken to start a business successfully. Click on *Entrepreneurs* for background information on a long list of people who have succeeded with their business start-ups:
http://www.startups.co.uk/

## Warm-up

Prepare your students for this exercise by forming them into small groups and giving them three minutes to brainstorm as long a list as possible of the personal qualities that it takes to be an entrepreneur. When the time is up, get your students to call out their suggestions and write these on the board assisting with formulation where necessary.

Now turn the students' attention to the quiz and ask what they think the title refers to. Give them five minutes to complete the quiz and tote up their scores with the aid of the key at the bottom of the page and the evaluation of results to the left of the page. Be prepared to explain the meaning of *persistence* and *diligence*. Next, bring the class back together and ask your students if any of them were surprised by their results: did students turn out to have the "Columbus spirit" who hadn't ever thought of themselves as potential entrepreneurs? Or the other way round. Had students gone into a different direction with their lists? You may decide to round off the activity by asking students to work with their neighbor to brainstorm other pertinent questions which might be added to the quiz. If you do this, allow just two to three minutes for the brainstorming before bringing the class back together and collecting suggestions on the board.

# 12 Starting a business

## Listening: Setting up a business

**1** Use these questions as a springboard to discuss the role universities play in fostering entrepreneurship. Extend the exercise by setting a further question: *does the university do enough to encourage and support entrepreneurship among students and in what ways could it do more?*

Write the students' examples about entrepreneurship on campus on the board assisting with formulation where necessary. Be sure to allow enough time to discuss whether your university does enough to foster entrepreneurship and get the students to cite specific examples of the type of additional support that could be offered to them. Encourage further discussion by putting a few additional questions. For instance, ask if students know of any business ideas that originated on (their) campus and if there are any joint ventures between their university and companies. You might also ask if your students would be interested in taking courses in entrepreneurship at university.

**2** Make it clear that they will have to manipulate the form of some of the words to complete the exercise successfully. They should work for two to three minutes on their own to fill in the gaps before you bring the class back together to collect answers.

1 Before going into production a <u>prototype</u> of the product has to be built.
2 The agency's superb marketing concept still needs to be <u>refined</u> to meet our specific needs.
3 Before starting your business, you are requested by law to <u>register</u> your company.
4 High <u>overheads</u>, such as rent and wages, can be a burden in the start-up phase of your business.
5 *BizOrg* sells a template which makes <u>devising</u> a business plan much easier.

**3** Ask your students to read the instructions, then ask them if they think there is anything surprising in the fact that such an ancient university hosts a conference on entrepreneurship. You may have to explain *Silicon Fen*: Cambridge lies in a flat, watery region of eastern England referred to as *the Fens*; the analogy is clearly with *Silicon Valley* in California.

Next, ask the students to read the questions and make it clear that they are to direct their listening only at the information they need to answer the questions. They should bear the questions in mind as they listen and write their answers in note form. Collect answers in open class.

1 Rebecca's business plan is to produce a network security product. She won the university's entrepreneur technology prize.
2 She has registered her company and they are going to launch the product in the next six months.
3 Rebecca wants to attract investment into her company.
4 She regards recession as a chance to develop her own ideas and learn new skills. She doesn't think there are many secure well-paid jobs at the moment.

**4** Use the questions here as an opportunity to get students thinking about the personal costs and benefits of entrepreneurship. Split the class into pairs and give your students the task of assessing the pros and cons of becoming an entrepreneur. They should use the factors listed under the question as a springboard for their discussions.

Students should have ten minutes for the pair work, then bring the class back together. Ask a pair to focus on one of the factors and the pros and cons they listed under it before moving on to the next pair and the next factor. Write the students' suggestions on the board.

**5** Form groups of four by quickly putting pairs together to tackle this question. Allow the students five minutes to brainstorm as long a list as possible of the factors that account for failure among start-ups. The five minutes of brainstorming over, bring the class back together and ask for a volunteer from each group to come to the board and write up the results of their brainstorming. Assist students with formulation of the points they write on the board where necessary.

There are a couple of reasons why so many start-ups fail within the first two to three years. Foremost are economic factors such as poor growth prospects and poor profitability. Both can be the result of tough economic times but also of poor planning and cost control. The latter happens when the business owner doesn't have the necessary management skills. So, it's definitely a good idea for students to get some expert advice before they think of opening up their own business.
Another stumbling block is the lack of capital and credit. Banks just don't like to lend money to small businesses, and other types of investors are hard to attract.
But some government agencies offer special funding for start-ups or recently founded businesses which offer long-term loans at very low interest rates and against little security.

# Starting a business    12

## Reading: **The Corporate Fitness Business Plan**

**1** Your students should work in their groups to consider the kind of information that potential investors would look for in a business plan. Prompt their thinking with a couple of additional questions: *Would investors only be interested in the financial side of a business plan* and *How important would the section of the plan concerned with market analysis be to investors?* Allow your students five minutes to come up with a list of questions before bringing the class back together to collect and discuss ideas.

> The kind of questions which potential investors may ask when looking at a business plan might include:
> - Do the people behind the plan have the right skills and experience to be successful?
> - Do they display a firm enough understanding of the market they are to work in?
> - Does the product/service feature enough USPs to differentiate it from its competitors?
> - Do projections of sales seem reasonable?
> - Is the financial risk going to be spread? Has the business already attracted other sources of finance?

**2** Your students should now read the business plan. Make it clear that their sole objective in this first read-through is to answer the two questions. They should acquaint themselves with these questions and bear them in mind while reading. They should not get bogged down in any vocabulary they don't understand but should take a note of this for later on. When they have finished reading, check answers in open class.

> 1 The start-up is registered but hasn't started operating so far. This is indicated by the start-up summary.
> 2 b

**3** Split your students into pairs to skim read the business plan more closely in order to consider which elements are missing from it. If an element which has been omitted from the plan occurs to a student during reading, they should suggest this to their other people in their group who should then read further to establish if this element has indeed been omitted. Allow your students five minutes to analyze the plan and decide what is missing before collecting their suggestions in open class.

> The business plan does not cover all aspects. The missing parts are: executive summary, financial plan and legal plan.

Now invite your students to explore the meaning of any vocabulary they didn't understand by sharing their knowledge with each other. Students should call out any words or expressions they don't understand. Write the terms on the board before inviting suggestions from other students as to what they mean. Clearly, you should be the final arbiter of what the definitions are and gently correct suggestions made by students which don't quite hit the mark. Be prepared to deal the words with *allocated*, *leasehold*, *expansion*, *incentive*, *accomplished* and *break-even point*.

**4** Finally, turn the group's attention to the first question under 4. They should consider this for a few minutes before making their suggestions to the class. Then ask students to complete the matching exercise. Tell them that if they have problems matching any of the terms to their definitions, they should find the words in the context of the business plan and decide which definitions are appropriate. Check answers in open class.

> 1 e, 2 g, 3 h, 4 b, 5 a, 6 c, 7 f

### Business plan word workout

> This photocopiable activity offers your students further exposure to key terminology from the business plan on page 116 of the Course Book and the opportunity to use the lexis in context.
>
> Split your students into pairs or groups of three so that you have an even number of groups. Give half of these the crossword A *Target language and clues* sheet and the other half the equivalent sheet for crossword B. Explain that the students are going to work with their partners to design a crossword puzzle. The words provided above the cutting line on their sheets are the key terms which are the solutions to their puzzles. Their task is to design clues which require these terms as answers: make it clear that the words must be used in the exact forms shown. To do this students should first return to the business plan on page 116 and find the words in context. They should then write gapped sentences as clues. Their sentences should be business plan-like but not identical to the sentences in the Course Book text. You may want to provide an example: to do this write *received* on the board and point out that the word is used in the business plan in the context of *received a university degree*. Now write the following sentence on the board:
>
> *Brian Norman _____ his MBA from the London School of Economics in 2007.*

# 12 Starting a business

Make it clear that this is the kind of clue you have in mind. Be on hand to assist students who have difficulty in writing their clues and have a look at all the clues to ensure that they are sound. Having written their clues, the students then tear off the bottom part of the sheet in preparation for the next stage.

Now team up all the pairs or groups with other pairs or groups and ask the students to swap their clues. At this point, hand out crosswords A and B to the appropriate groups or pairs and allow the students five minutes to solve their crosswords. They should do this, in the first instance without referring to the Course Book text but can obviously have a look if they get stuck. Round off by confirming the correct answers and encourage students to record the terms in their vocabulary notebooks.

## Discussion: Assessing the economic viability of a business idea

**1** Divide your students into groups and ask them to read the instructions. In their groups they should scrutinize the business plan for the information required in the checklist. Allow up to 15 minutes for this so that the students can go into real detail in their discussions. When this phase is over, bring the class back together and ask two or three students from different groups to summarize the information they have gleamed from the business plan in answer to the points on the check list. Invite students to correct one another's perceptions about what is stated in the business plan.

**2** Ask if anyone can describe how a SWOT analysis works. Students who did the SWOT analysis in the *Over to you* section in Unit 1 can be asked to explain what a SWOT analysis is about and how it might be useful in this context. SWOT stands for *strengths*, *weaknesses*, *opportunities* and *threats*; the students should think about the proposed business idea from these perspectives and make four lists under each of the headings.

As the students complete the SWOT analysis, go round the class prompting groups with questions, i.e. *So, do you see the fact that the business model is new here as a strength or a weakness?* and assisting with formulation.

> Note the subjective nature of a SWOT analysis and that there are no right or wrong answers. The main object of the exercise is that any ultimate decision to invest is based on thorough scrutiny of the business proposal.

**3** Tell the groups that they should feed the results of this discussion back to the class: they should organize their arguments in clear notes, making reference to the result of their SWOT analysis. You could point out that they may decide to allocate only some of the $100,000 to the business. In this case they will have to account for why they reached the decision to allocate less funding and the perceived risks they took into consideration when doing this. Prompt their thinking about the kind of conditions that might be linked to lending the money by asking for a few examples from the class before the discussion begins. Conditions here might include, for instance, an executive seat on the board, stringent repayment conditions in advance of clear profitability, a percentage of future profits and/or a preferential stake in the business should the company undertake an IPO.

Allow up to ten minutes for the groups to complete their deliberations before bringing the class back together and asking each group in turn to present their decision and the detailed reasoning which underpins this.

### Business Skills

## Executive summaries: What are the key issues?

**1** Ask your students to read the instructions and check that they understand the task by asking for a volunteer to explain what the purpose of an executive summary is as well as what it contains. Ask another student to explain what they are to do with the text. Make sure that students understand that their task is to summarize the contents of each section of the executive summary using key words. Allow between five and ten minutes for the completion of the exercise before bringing the class back together to check answers. You might do this by quickly drawing the flow chart on the board and asking for three volunteers to fill in each section. Allow other students to make their own suggestions as to which key words best describe a sections content. Ensure students have enough time to discuss what an executive summary contains and understand the terminology used.

# Starting a business  12

| Introduction | Marketing potential | Financial summary |
|---|---|---|
| • *start-up business* | • *competition* | • *break-even-point* |
| • *objective of the business* | • *target group* | • *sale (year one)* |
| • *requirements for operation* | • *development of the market* | • *expenses (year one)* |
|  | • *marketing strategy* | • *net income (before tax)* |
|  |  | • *return on equity (ROE)* |

**2** Save valuable classroom time by setting this task as homework. Make it clear that, as well as referring to their completed flowcharts, the students should identify phrases or "chunks" of language such as sentence heads, i. e. *Based on ...; The project will require an initial investment of ...,* from *The Circle's* executive summary to help them write their executive summary. Ask your students to send you their work in advance of the next lesson so that you can comment upon it. When commenting upon and correcting the executive summaries target your remarks at the structure, the use of key terminology and of the phrases. At the next lesson, hand back the students' work with your corrections and suggestions. Invite the students to read these in their own time and come back to you with questions later on. Ask the students to swap the printouts they have brought to class with the person sitting next to them. They are to read their partner's work and comment upon the aspects of it that they feel are particularly successful. Allow up to 20 minutes for this and circulate, listening in on discussions and sparingly offering your own comments.

## Using legal terminology: Describing a company's legal structure

**1** Explain to your students that they are now going to acquaint themselves with some important terminology which is clearly related to the topic of the unit. Any discussion about business start up demands at least a basic knowledge of the various options for company structure. Additionally, point out that the lexis here will assist them with the following reading exercise. Allow them five minutes to complete the matching of terms and definitions before checking answers in open class.

1 b, 2 e, 3 a, 4 d, 5 g, 6 f, 7 h, 8 c

**2** You may decide to save class time by setting this reading as homework in which case you should discuss answers with the class at the next lesson.

Alternatively, you could carry out the reading as collaborative, communicative activity. To do this, carry out a brief session of brainstorming with the whole class in order to establish what students already know about the various company types: write suggestions on the board. Then split your students into groups of three assigning each group member one of the company types to work on. Try to assign *limited liability companies* to the strongest reader in each group. Allow between five and ten minutes for reading and questions before asking the students to work within their groups to exchange the information they have gathered from the texts in answer to the questions. The students should take notes of what their partners explain to them.

Now bring the class back together and ask students to provide answers for a company type which they read about. Where necessary, invite other students to supplement this with further information from the texts. Continue this until all of the information for each company type has been provided.

You may decide to extend the exercise by asking students to consider the pros and cons of the various legal forms. To do this, return your students to their groups – you might speed matters up by assigning groups with one specific legal form to discuss – asking them to list as many pros and cons as possible. When the students have completed their discussion, bring the class back together and consolidate their suggestions on the board.

Conclude by drawing attention to the language box on page 119 which contrasts British and American terminology and encourage students to record this in their vocabulary notebooks.

# 12 Starting a business

**3** Focus your students on their first listening task by making it clear that they are only to listen for information about the legal structure of each company on this first run-through of the CD track. Collect answers in open class.

> Adrian Harris, *Dream Cars Europe:* Private limited company
> Ken and Bobby, *Skateboarding.com:* Partnership
> Gareth Evans, *Marketingonline:* Sole trader
> Helen Stuart, *Stuart Homes:* Public limited company

Before playing the CD track again, ask your students to spend a few moments taking notes about any advantages or disadvantages of the various legal forms which they might remember. Now play the CD again, instructing your students to listen in order to check if their recollections proved correct and to note down further advantages and disadvantages.

> **Private limited company:** liability restricted, good for risky business partners need to provide necessary capital; more legal duties
> **Partnership:** business is easy to run, partners can share experiences and support each other all partners fully liable, disagreement could end the partnership
> **Sole trader:** owner remains independent, business is easy to run, suitable for businesses which don't need large investments; owner fully liable
> **Public limited company:** liability restricted, suitable when a lot of capital is needed more legal duties, corporation tax

## Ups and downs in business

> This photocopiable board game will test your students' knowledge of the legal forms of companies in the U.K. which they read about on pages 119 and 120 of the Course Book.
>
> To use it pair off your students, giving each one board game, two counters and a coin. Explain the rules. The first player tosses the coin: heads = move two spaces; tails = move one. ('Tails' is the side which shows the value of the coin.) When a player lands on a text space, they must say which type or types of company the statement applies to. If they get this right, they stay on the same space and the next player takes their turn. If they get it wrong, they move back one space. If a player lands on a climbing space, they climb up and address the statement in the square at the top. If they do this correctly, they may stay there. If not, they must climb back down. If a player lands on a skiing space, they ski down and address the statement at the bottom. If they do this correctly, they may stay there. If not, they must go back one space. The winner is the first player to reach the last square.

Create movement in the classroom by attaching a copy of the answer key to the board. Make it clear that students can refer to this if they want to dispute an answer given by their playing partner. However, they have a maximum of ten seconds to make the trip to the board to check the answer, their partner should keep time.

Be sure to spend a few minutes once the game is over confirming the correct answers for the class.

Key:
1   PLC
2   Sole trader and Partnership
4   Ltd. and PLC
5   Sole trader and Partnership
6   Ltd.
8   Sole trader, Partnership and Ltd.
9   PLC
10  Sole trader
12  Ltd. and PLC
13  Sole trader and partnership
16  PLC
17  Sole trader and Partnership
18  Ltd. and PLC

## Company Case: **The pitfalls of franchising**

Ensure that all your students understand the meaning of *pitfalls* by asking if someone can explain the term. Then ask the class to brainstorm what the potential pitfalls of franchising might be. Note the students' suggestions on the board. Rather than this being an exercise in creating a list of realistic pitfalls, the object here is to prepare the students for the reading they are to do, so go easy on any of the suggestions which don't seem to be realistic to you.

Next ask your students to read over the text. They should adopt a skim reading approach in order to identify the sections of the text which are concerned with the problems that arise for Tom. They should then read these sections closely. Having given the students some five minutes to complete the reading, ask them which particular pitfalls Tom experiences in the arrangement with Heuriger. Write these on the board. Conclude this phase – and prepare your students for the kind of thinking they're going to be doing in the next phase – by asking for two or three suggestions as to what Tom might do. The object of this is to provide a small number of possible courses of action by way of example: as the students will have to come up with and discuss more of the like on their own next, don't spend too long on this.

Now split your students into groups and name each of these after a well-known consultancy: *McKinsey and Company, The*

# Starting a business 12

*Boston Consulting Group, Deloitte Consulting, PricewaterhouseCoopers* and so on. Tell the groups that they have up to 20 minutes to arrive at a strategy which Tom could adopt to deal with the difficulties his brand is experiencing. As the groups will have to present their ideas to the class, encourage the students to spend the last five minutes preparing this presentation so that it has a clear structure. As the students discuss the strategies they are going to propose, circulate and chip in your own suggestions if you feel that a group needs a little prompting. There are a variety of options open to Tom which you might suggest to get students thinking. He could, for instance, leverage his legal agreement with Heuriger and sue him into compliance with his brand values, initiate a PR offensive to distance his brand from the troubled coffeeshops elsewhere or, as a last resort, consider re-branding his business. As you listen in on discussions, take notes of any mistakes you hear to feed back to the class for self-correction later on.

When the discussion time is over, invite each group of consultants to make their presentation. Once this is over, hold a free vote in order to give the class a chance to decide which consulting group Tom should choose to deal with his problems.

Finally, write any mistakes that you noted during the discussion on the board and invite the class to correct them. Be sure not to identify the originators of the mistakes when doing so.

## Over to you

### Project: Developing a business idea

Inject some fun into this exercise – and ensure that your students will complete it – by telling them that they will present their business idea to potential investors at a meeting of *First Tuesday* at the next lesson. Explain that *First Tuesday* is a networking forum for people with business ideas (particularly in the new media sector) and potential investors. The event, held on the first Tuesday of each month in major cities across the world, was used by entrepreneurs during the first internet boom to drum up funding for their businesses.

The students' task is to think of a product or service and then concoct a brief, punchy sales pitch of no longer than one minute which they will make repeatedly to "investors" at the next lesson. Despite the time limit, students should attempt to condense all the information asked for in the Course Book into their pitches. At the lesson, have the students circulate and make their pitch individually to their classmates. When this is over, allow the students to vote on which idea they liked best.

### Web research: Finding out about funding possibilities for start-ups

Advise your students to start their searches on the websites of their city and state administrations.

Encourage everyone to undertake the research by telling the students that you will be spending some time at the next class discussing their results.

### Reading: Campus dragons

1. Spurred on by popular TV programs about entrepreneurialism, British students are currently interested in becoming entrepreneurs either in order to avoid working for big companies or to improve their skills in advance of getting a job with a large employer.
2. Warwick University has fostered this trend by staging an annual competition in which student entrepreneurs compete to be awarded prizes for their business ideas.
4. Entrants were required to submit a 250-word business plan. Judges chose the best four ideas and the entrepreneurs behind these then had to write and pitch a business proposal to the judges.
5. The first prize was £1,000, the second £250.

# Photocopiable activity 1 — Sentence Auction

| Correct the mistakes | Bid ($1,500 total) |
|---|---|
| I would like applying for an internship with your company. | |
| I was born on 17 of August 1985. | |
| After leaving school, I was doing a training program in IT. | |
| I have done an internship with IBM last year. | |
| At the moment, I study business administration. | |
| I am looking forward to hear from you. | |
| As part of my internship, I worked on the Marketing department. | |
| I studied business at the University of South-west South Dakota since 2008. | |

Photocopiable activity 2 **So, can we agree to that?**

| Suggesting | |
|---|---|
| Why | don't we … |
| Wouldn't it be better | if we … |
| How | about if we … |

| Looking for agreement | |
|---|---|
| Well, I think we can both agree | on … |
| Could we both go | along with … |
| Can we | agree to … |

| Rejecting a suggestion | |
|---|---|
| I don't think I can go | along with that. |
| I'm not sure I can agree | to that. |
| I really can't | agree on that. |

| Asking for clarification | |
|---|---|
| How might | this work? |
| Could you explain that | a bit further? |
| Can you run that | by me again, please? |

| Rounding up | |
|---|---|
| Can we leave | it here, then? |
| So, let's go | with that idea, shall we? |
| Good. That's | settled then. |

# 2 Photocopiable activity 3 Email puzzle

**Email A**

| From: | |
| To: | |
| Cc: | |
| Subject: | |

| | |
|---|---|
| Hello Joanna | |
| Thanks for getting | back to me so quickly. |
| I'm sorry, but the date you've suggested is not going to | work after all. |
| Unfortunately, everyone else | has cancelled. |
| I have to find a new date | that suits everyone. |
| Would you be able to meet the following week | on the 29th at 10.30? |
| Or how about 4 October | at 9.00 a.m.? |
| Please let me know which date | works best for you as soon as you can. |
| Hope to hear | from you soon. |
| All the | best |

102

## Photocopiable activity 4  Email puzzle

**Email B**

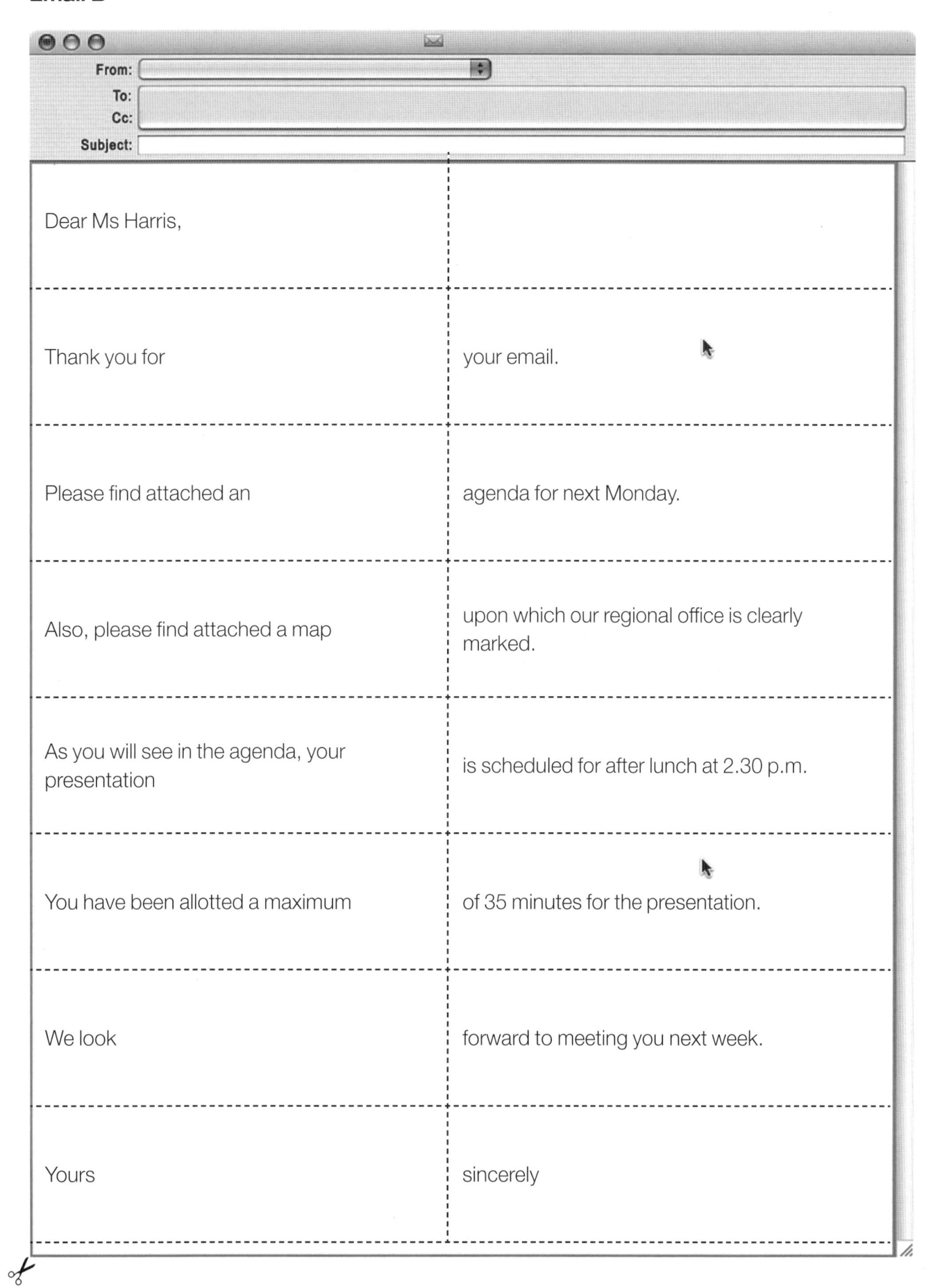

| From: | |
| To: | |
| Cc: | |
| Subject: | |

| | |
|---|---|
| Dear Ms Harris, | |
| Thank you for | your email. |
| Please find attached an | agenda for next Monday. |
| Also, please find attached a map | upon which our regional office is clearly marked. |
| As you will see in the agenda, your presentation | is scheduled for after lunch at 2.30 p.m. |
| You have been allotted a maximum | of 35 minutes for the presentation. |
| We look | forward to meeting you next week. |
| Yours | sincerely |

103

# 3 Photocopiable activity 4 — Teleshopping

| | |
|---|---|
| Good afternoon. Home from Home Furnishings. Frazer speaking. How can I help you? | Hi. I've just been trying to place an order on your website but it won't work. |
| Ah. I'm sorry about that. We have a problem with our website at the moment. But it will be working again in a couple of hours. | Well. That is too bad. I wanted to place my order now while I have some time. |
| I do apologize. I can understand you're upset. If you like, you could place your order with me now on the telephone. | Mmm. I wanted to order online but OK. I'd like to order the Pikig sofa – in red. Is it in stock? |
| Let me see. Yes, we have one in red for you. Now, is this your first order with us? | Yes, it is. |
| In that case I would need your name and address. | Sure. My name is Tom Fisher. That's F-i-s-h-e-r. |
| OK. And what's your shipping address, Mr Fisher? | It's 37 High Tree Road, Oxford, OX7 3GP. |
| Sorry, I didn't get your post code. Could you spell that out for me, please? | Of course. The postcode is O-X-7 3-G-P. |
| Let me read that back to you: Tom Fisher, 37 High Tree Road, Oxford, OX7 3GP. | Yes, that's correct. |
| OK, I've got that. Now I need your credit card details. What kind of credit card do you want to use? | It's a Visa card. |
| Could you give me the number, please? | It's 2572 0032 2566 0066. |
| And the security code and expiration date? | Ehm … 406 and September 2018. |
| Thank you very much. We'll be dispatching your sofa to you within 24 hours. Is there anything else I can do for you now, Mr Fisher? | No, thank you. |
| Well, thank you for calling. Have a great day! | Same to you. Bye. |
| Goodbye. | |

Photocopiable activity 5 — **Telephone performance – A manager's evaluation**

## Conversation 1

Customer repeatedly connected with the wrong telephone support agent.

Agent, on occasion, didn't sound interested in the customer.

Support agent could benefit from further training in how to explain technical issues in non-technical language.

Lack of courtesy – for example, agent interrupts customer.

Failure to apologize to customer or offer alternatives.

Too direct – not "diplomatic" enough – when questioning customer about problem.

## Conversation 2

Takes too long to pick up the call then speaks unclearly.

Tries to get customer off the phone almost immediately.

Agent seems distracted and to be doing something else in the background.

Fails to ask the customer about exact needs.

Inconsistency – agent says they will make an appointment for customer, then wants to connect customer with someone else.

Annoys customer with a direct question then repeats the question instead of rewording it.

## Red herrings

Confuses the customer by offering far too many options.

Makes inappropriate personal remarks about the customer.

Admits the company is at fault too early in call without finding out enough about the problem.

# Photocopiable activity 6  Retailing race board game

**Phrase cards**

| | |
|---|---|
| Customers may/might be tempted to … | Retailers may/might be tempted to … |
| Consumers may/might wonder whether … | Retailers may/might wonder whether … |
| Consumers may/might conclude that … | Retailers may/might conclude that … |
| Retailers could/will probably … | Customers could/will probably … |
| Retailers may/might hope for … | Customers may/might hope for … |

## Photocopiable activity 6 — Retailing race board game

| 16 **Miss a turn** | 17 Swap places on the board with one of your competitors. | 18 | **Finish** |
|---|---|---|---|
| 15 **Move to the next square** | 14 Fast food retailer MacBurger apologizes for trying to cover up an outbreak of food poisoning. | 13 The government increases VAT rates to 7.5 and 20%. | 12 The British government confirms rumors of a fresh outbreak of "mad cow disease". |
| 8 The government announces a ban on the import of clothing manufactured using child labor. | 9 | 10 A major new report links screen radiation from iPhones to brain tumors. | 11 A large U.S. bike manufacturer launches an electric bike which can reach speeds of 45 km per hour and retails for under $500. |
| 7 | 6 The Central Bank announces a 1% rise in interest rates. | 5 **Move to the next square** | 4 A US supermarket giant announces plans to enter the food retailing market |
| **Start** | 1 Changes in credit law make credit cards more widely available. | 2 Amazon.com, the online retailer, collapses overnight. | 3 |

# Photocopiable activity 7 — Solving a problem by phone

| | |
|---|---|
| OneWorld Freight. Sara Jones speaking. How can I help you? | Hello. This is Ross Brothers at Harvolux in Milton Keynes. I have a problem with a shipment you're taking care of for us. Could you help me with that? |
| Sure, Mr Brothers. I'll see what I can do. Can you tell me what the problem is with the shipment? | Well actually, it's not with the shipment but with the bill of lading. I'm afraid there are one or two mistakes on it that I need to clear up quickly. |
| I'm really sorry about that. Can you give me the bill of lading number first of all? | Sure, it's 43898. |
| OK. I've got that. Now, let me see. OK. Can you tell me what the problem is? | Right, well, to start with the company name of the consignee is unfortunately wrong. It should be Adelbax S.A. but I'm afraid that on the bill of lading it says Adellax Ltd. |
| Oh right. I am sorry about that. I'll change it immediately. Now, was there anything else? | Yes, there was. The bill of lading says that the weight of our shipment was 250 lbs. I'm sorry, but that isn't true. The shipment weighs just 25 lbs. |
| I'm sorry, Mr Brothers. Let me apologize for that. I can see from your original email here that the weight is 25 lbs. Look, I'll correct these mistakes on the bill of lading immediately. | Great. Thank you. |
| I'll send out a corrected copy of the bill of lading to you by post this afternoon. Let me just say sorry again. I hope this hasn't inconvenienced you too much. | Not at all. Thank you for your help. Goodbye. |
| Thank you for calling, Mr Brothers. Goodbye. | |

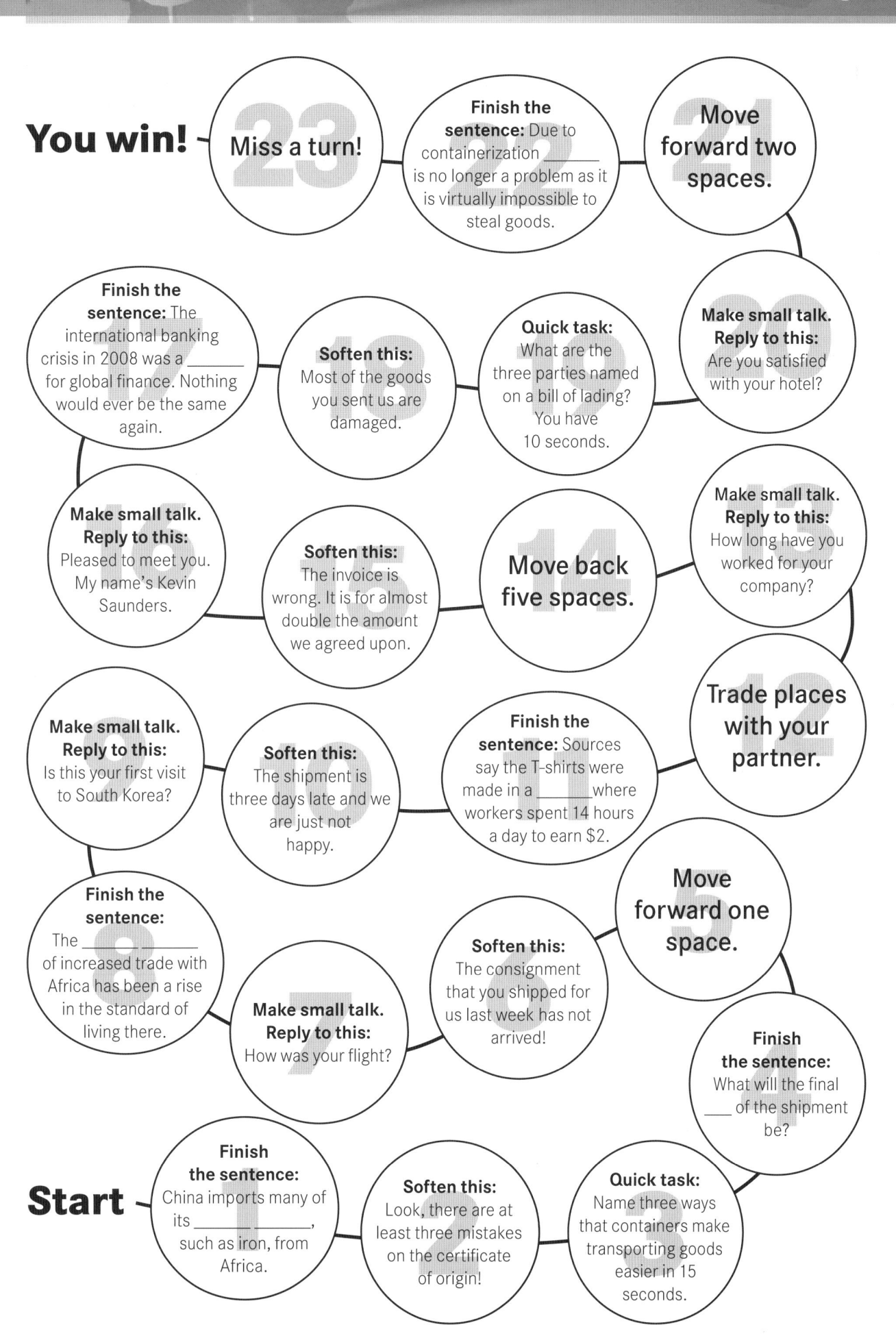

Photocopiable activity 8  **Trade talk board game**

**You win!**

**23** Miss a turn!

**22** Finish the sentence: Due to containerization _____ is no longer a problem as it is virtually impossible to steal goods.

**21** Move forward two spaces.

**17** Finish the sentence: The international banking crisis in 2008 was a _____ for global finance. Nothing would ever be the same again.

**18** Soften this: Most of the goods you sent us are damaged.

**19** Quick task: What are the three parties named on a bill of lading? You have 10 seconds.

**20** Make small talk. Reply to this: Are you satisfied with your hotel?

**16** Make small talk. Reply to this: Pleased to meet you. My name's Kevin Saunders.

**15** Soften this: The invoice is wrong. It is for almost double the amount we agreed upon.

**14** Move back five spaces.

**13** Make small talk. Reply to this: How long have you worked for your company?

**9** Make small talk. Reply to this: Is this your first visit to South Korea?

**10** Soften this: The shipment is three days late and we are just not happy.

**11** Finish the sentence: Sources say the T-shirts were made in a _____ where workers spent 14 hours a day to earn $2.

**12** Trade places with your partner.

**8** Finish the sentence: The _____ of increased trade with Africa has been a rise in the standard of living there.

**7** Make small talk. Reply to this: How was your flight?

**6** Soften this: The consignment that you shipped for us last week has not arrived!

**5** Move forward one space.

**4** Finish the sentence: What will the final ___ of the shipment be?

**Start**

**1** Finish the sentence: China imports many of its _____, such as iron, from Africa.

**2** Soften this: Look, there are at least three mistakes on the certificate of origin!

**3** Quick task: Name three ways that containers make transporting goods easier in 15 seconds.

109

# Photocopiable activity 9  Manufacturing keywords board game

| 16 **Problems downstream** – go back two spaces. | 17 **What's the word?** The components and raw materials currently in store. | 18 **Finish the sentence:** *This is the section of the ____ line where we fit the wheels to the car.* | **You win!** |
|---|---|---|---|
| 15 **Push production** – you have 20 seconds to describe what this is. | 14 **Downtime!** Miss a turn | 13 **Waste** – you have 20 seconds to identify the seven types. | 12 **Production in sequence** – you have 20 seconds to describe what this is. |
| 8 **Problems downstream** – go back three spaces. | 9 **What's the word?** The area where products are manufactured in a factory. | 10 **Downstream process** – you have 20 seconds to describe what this is. | 11 **Downtime!** Miss a turn. |
| 7 **Pull production** – you have 20 seconds to describe what this is. | 6 **What's the word?** An imperfection in an object or machine. | 5 **Downtime!** Miss a turn. | 4 **What's the word?** All the people who work for a company. |
| **Start** | 1 **Upstream process** – you have ten seconds to describe what this is. | 2 **Finish the sentence:** *We have to constantly refine our processes as ____ times are getting shorter.* | 3 **Lean production** – you have 20 seconds to describe what this is. |

| target | audience |
| sporting | events |
| gaming | environment |
| sponsorship | fees |
| official | sponsor |
| promotional | strategy |
| low | budget |
| embedded | advertising |
| advertising | strategy |
| promotion | method |

# 7 Photocopiable activity 11 Strategic Presentation workout

Good morning, ladies and gentlemen.

My name's Sally Andrews and I'm the Account Director at Burtley North Advertising.

Burtley North is a small advertising agency but we've developed a reputation for helping companies with no experience of advertising on the internet get their online advertising campaigns going.

Thank you for giving me the chance to talk to you about your brand and how we can help develop it online.

Let me start by giving you an overview of what I'm going to say this afternoon.

To begin with, I'll give you a better idea of the kind of internet advertising campaigns we've been involved in. I'm sure you're going to be impressed by our list of clients and how we've helped them.

The second part of my presentation will be an analysis of the kind of advertising you've been doing so far.

Next, I'll outline the campaign that we've developed for you and explain where we would run your ads on the internet.

Finally, I'll be giving you a demonstration of some of the animated banner adverts we've designed for you.

My presentation will take about half an hour. If you have any questions, I'll be happy to answer them at the end.

Right. Let's start. I want to tell you about …

---

**Student A**

Name – Use your own name
Job – Sales manager
Company – SlipStream Sports Sponsorship

**Presentation subject – Sponsoring the Children's Football World Cup**

Presentation structure:
1 – The history of the Children's Football World Cup
2 – An overview of companies which already sponsor the event
3 – The choice of sponsorship packages

**Student B**

Name – Use your own name
Job – Marketing manager
Company – Clear Text Office Printers

**Presentation subject – Our new low-cost G3 Office Printer and how we're going to market it**

Presentation structure:
1 – The advantages of the G3 over other similar products
2 – An overview of our marketing campaign and which media we will use
3 – A demonstration of the advertisement which will be run on television and the internet

## Photocopiable activity 12 — Negotiating the best deal

| | |
|---|---|
| Come in, Ms de Bonville. Please take a seat. | Thanks. It's good of you to take the time to see me this morning. |
| Not at all. Now, you said on the phone that you have $150,000 to invest. | Right. And as this is the bank I do most of my business with, I thought I'd come to you first. Basically, I want to invest the money in a high-interest environment … I want a high-yield return on the cash as quickly as possible. |
| OK. I'd recommend commercial paper to you then. I could offer you Dell and BP, for instance. They offer a high yield with little in the way of risk. The current average yield is 4.9% for a six month lifespan. | That sounds pretty good. What about fees though? |
| Well, we take a commission of 0.3%. We need to do this to pay the brokerage charges we incur in supplying the commercial paper. There's also a one-off administration fee of $830. | Look, you know how much business I do with your bank. And that I've banked with you for years. So, I feel that you could be making a better offer. |
| OK. I hear what you're saying. I could reduce the commission to 0.25% | Alright. I would find 0.2% more acceptable. But only with the additional provision that I don't pay the administration fee. |
| Hmm. OK. I could make an exception in your case and waive the administration fee. But with regard to the commission, I can't go lower than 0.24%. | I'm afraid that won't really do. |
| OK. What do you have in mind, then? | 2.2%. |
| Alright. 2.3%. But I can only offer you this on the understanding that you continue to do business with us to the extent that you have done in the past. | Yes, of course. Right. That's a deal, then. |
| I certainly think so. OK, so let's go over what we've agreed. | |

# Photocopiable activity 13 — Organigram puzzle

| | |
|---|---|
| Moyra Evans is in charge of the whole show. | Roger Conibear is ultimately in charge of Tina Dean. |
| Both Pat Moor and Gavin de Carl report directly to Susan Tatum. | Tina Dean works for Claire Crawford. |
| Susan Tatum takes overall responsibility for the revenue-generating side of the business. | Claire Crawford manages the personnel side of the business. |
| Andy Gorman is responsible for selling advertising on a day-to-day basis. | Brenda Fricker works ultimately under the direction of Roger Conibear. |
| Gill McNeish has the same responsibilities as Andy Gorman and reports directly to Gavin de Carl. | Karen Brian is one of George Stoke's direct reports. |
| Aurindam Majumdar heads up the business's technical operations. | Stephen Forbes is responsible for developing software solutions on a day-to-day basis. |
| Nick Sykes is directly accountable to Moyra Evans. | Kim Slattery reports to the same manager as Stephen Forbes. |
| Nial Mitchell's manager reports directly to Nick Sykes. | |

## Photocopiable activity 14 — Meeting phrases matching game

| | |
|---|---|
| Can we get started? | Let's get down to business, shall we? |
| I'm afraid I have to apologize for Anita Gupta. | Claire Bolderson sends her apologies. |
| I think we can expect this first session to take until … | We'll probably have dealt with this issue by … |
| I think you are all familiar with the agenda. | You're all up to speed with what we're here to talk about today. |
| Could we give you the floor? | Can I hand over now to you? |
| And now I'd like to come to the central item on the agenda. | Right, I'd like to move onto our main business now. |
| We'll be breaking for coffee around … | We'll take a comfort break at … |
| There will be plenty of time for your questions and comments later. | We'll pick up on any points you want to make soon. |
| Could I have your attention please? | Can I bring you to order, please? |
| Let's take it in turns. | One at a time, please. |

# Worldcon reports record rise in earnings – for the third year running

## Companies under too much pressure to boost shareholder value, warns report

## Andersen: "Staffers worked into the night covering up the Enron trail"

## Do the numbers add up? – U.S. legislators call for personal responsibility in the boardroom

## New regulatory body to be given wide ranging powers over auditing firms

## Business is booming – CPAs can choose their employer and name their price

## Smaller public companies groaning under the cost burden of reporting standards, warn business leaders

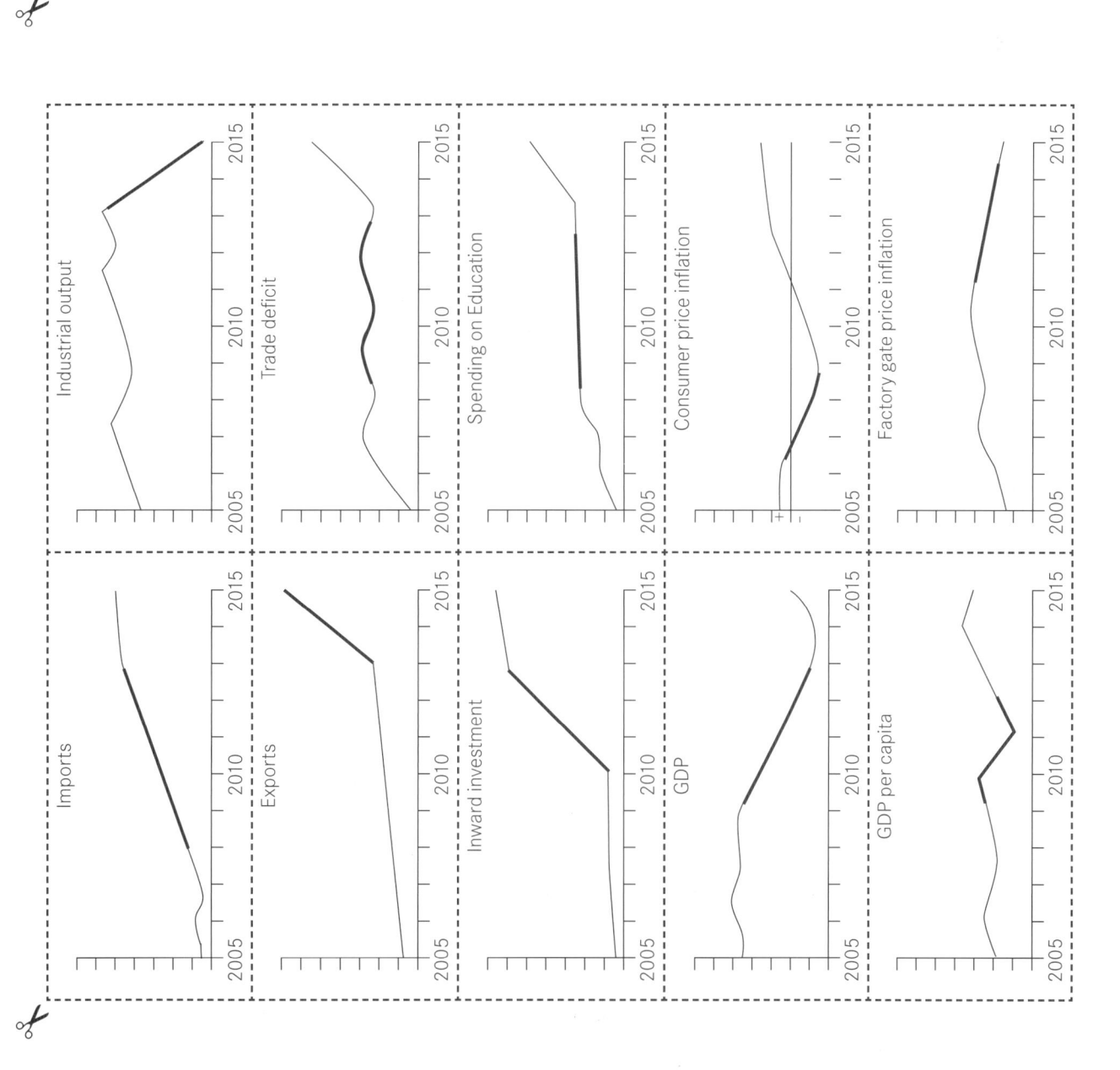

**Photocopiable activity 16  Describing trends card game**

| ... increased dramatically ... | ... increased sharply ... | ... rocketed to ... | ... fell dramatically ... | ... fell sharply ... | ... plummeted... | ... fluctuated around ... | ... remained stable at ... | ... negative growth of ... | ... declined gradually ... |

| Industrial output | Trade deficit | Spending on Education | Consumer price inflation | Factory gate price inflation |

| Imports | Exports | Inward investment | GDP | GDP per capita |

# 12 Photocopiable activity 17  Business plan word workout

## Crossword A

### Target language and clues

These are the target words you have to create clues for:

**Across**

3. even
6. integral
7. requires

**Down**

1. headquarters
2. comparable
4. founders
5. mission
8. accomplish

---

**Across**

3. _____

6. _____

7. _____

**Down**

1. _____

2. _____

4. _____

5. _____

8. _____

Photocopiable activity 17  **Business plan word workout**  **12**

## Crossword A

Crossword A

119

# Photocopiable activity 17 — Business plan word workout

## Crossword B

**Target language and clues**

These are the target words you have to create clues for:

### Across
1. headed
6. convince
7. oversees
8. indicates

### Down
2. allocated
3. target
4. earned
5. ownership

---

### Across

1. _____

6. _____

7. _____

8. _____

### Down

2. _____

3. _____

4. _____

5. _____

Photocopiable activity 17 **Business plan word workout** 12

**Crossword B**

121

## 12 Photocopiable activity 18  Ups and downs in business

| 16 Can't trade without first issuing £50,000 in shares | 17 In the event of problems, home and possessions may be at risk | 18 Must be incorporated at Companies House | **Finish** |
|---|---|---|---|
| 15 | 14 | 13 Personal responsibility for debts run up by the business | 12 In event of profitability, corporation tax is due |
| 8 Can't offer shares on the stock market | 9 Must have a qualified company secretary | 10 Any profits go to you | 11 |
| 7 | 6 Can have one or more members | 5 Annual self-assessment tax return to HMRC is required | 4 Has to file accounts with Companies House |
| **Start** | 1 Has to publish accounts | 2 Money raised for the business from personal assets and/or loans | 3 |

UNIVERSITY OF SUSSEX

SCLS

LLC LANGUAGE TUTOR REFERENCE